W9-BTG-422

E. E. Cummings : A Bibliography

GEORGE J. FIRMAGE

E. E. CUMMINGS:
A BIBLIOGRAPHY

WESLEYAN UNIVERSITY PRESS

Middletown, Connecticut

ALSO BY GEORGE J. FIRMAGE
A Checklist of the Published Writings of Gertrude Stein
(Amherst, Mass., 1954)
E. E. *Cummings: A Miscellany* (New York, 1958)

Library of Congress Catalog Card Number: 60-7257
Manufactured in the United States of America
First edition

Contents

Preface

THE PUBLICATION of *E. E. Cummings: A Bibliography* follows closely upon the heels of Cummings' sixty-fifth birthday and is, first of all, a belated tribute to that cause for celebration. It also represents nearly fifteen years of reading and collecting the published work of Cummings; more than five years of recording and collating the material that is included in the present volume; the groundwork for the publication, two years ago, of *E. E. Cummings: A Miscellany*; and a friendship that began one January afternoon in 1957 when the present writer was invited to Patchin Place to discuss his work-in-progress over a cup of hearty tea.

This bibliography, like any bibliography of a living author, cannot make claims to completeness; it is and, let us hope, will remain a "work-in-progress" for many years to come. However, for the period covered, every effort has been made to make it as inclusive as possible. A number of documents relating to the publication of books and pamphlets by Cummings as well as actual appearances in magazines and newspapers have already been lost or destroyed. Perhaps the "lost" documents and appearances will someday be found. In the meantime, I hope the present study, even with its omissions, will fill the need for a bibliography of Cummings.[1]

This book is concerned only with the published work of its "non-hero" [2] and follows, except in the instances noted below, standard bibliographical practices.

1. Paul Lauter's *E. E. Cummings: Index to First Lines and Bibliography of Work By and About the Poet* was, to quote its author, "conceived and executed as a research tool and not primarily as a descriptive bibliography." Its value, even as a "research tool," is marred by many inaccuracies and omissions.
2. Secondary material has been treated in detail by my friend S. V. Baum,

E. E. Cummings

EXCEPTION 1: Page measurements in inches have been substituted for the height of the binding in centimeters.

EXCEPTION 2: Only books *by* Cummings are described in detail.

EXCEPTION 3: In quoting first lines of poems, a single slant (/) has been used to indicate a typographical separation of the line's elements; e.g.:

a. for 'a/mong crum/bling people(a'
   read 'a

        mong crum

                bling people(a'

b. for 'the/ sky/ was'
   read 'the

        sky

          was'.

When two poems have identical first lines, a double slant (//) has been used to indicate the presence of a second line; e.g.:

a. for 'listen// beloved'
   read 'listen
        beloved'

b. for 'listen// this a dog barks and'
   read 'listen
        this a dog barks and'

Without the aid and enthusiastic support of Mr. Cummings and his wife, the photographer Marion Morehouse, *E. E. Cummings: A Bibliography* would have little claim to comprehensiveness, let alone to authority. To both of them my sincerest thanks for their help, patience, and understanding.

Many others have helped me in my search for appearances, translations, publication records, musical settings of poems, and recordings made by Cummings. For the use of material in their possession, and for information leading to the discovery of unlisted appearances, my thanks go to Jeanne Ballot, Copy Executive for Condé Nast Publications; S. V. Baum, Instructor in English at Temple University; Eugene Delafield, New York bibliophile; Norman Friedman, Instructor in English at the University of Connecticut; Donald Gallup, Curator of the American Literature Collection at Yale University Library; Lorraine Rothbard Gleckman, editor and publisher of *diameter*; Gerald

---

whose *RE:eec*, a collection of critical essays and reviews together with a bibliographical appendix of secondary source material, awaits publication.

Preface

Gross, book editor and Cummings enthusiast; D. Jon Grossman, Cummings' authorized French translator; Carl K. Hersey, Chairman of the Department of Fine Arts at the University of Rochester; S. A. Jacobs, "poemprinter"; Charles Norman, author of *The Magic-Maker, E. E. Cummings*; Tony Saltzman, editor of *The Ottawa Hills Spectator*; Charles Schlessiger, assistant to Cummings' former agent at Brandt & Brandt; Pauline H. Turkel, editor and publisher of *In Memory of Fitzi*; and Robert A. Wilson, New York book collector and bibliophile. For translations of Cummings' appearances in Japanese, Arabic, Persian, Danish, Swedish, and Norwegian, I am indebted to Mrs. Kazuko M. Dailey, of the Industrial Bank of Japan Ltd.; Khalil Itani, of the United Nations' Translation Department; M. H. Sadri, of the Bank of Melli, Iran; and Ragnhild Sierveld, of the Translators Department of the First National City Bank of New York. For supplying information about material in their collections, I thank the staffs of the New York Public Library, the Library of Congress, and the university and college libraries at Buffalo, Columbia, Harvard, Hobart and William Smith, Ohio State, Temple, Vermont, and Yale. Publication facts and figures have been supplied by the Argophile Press; Duell, Sloan & Pearce; The Golden Eagle Press; Grove Press; Harcourt, Brace & Company; Harvard University Press; Henry Holt & Company; Jonathan Cape; Liveright Publishing Corporation; The Macmillan Company; The National Council of Teachers of English; Oxford University Press; Random House; and William Sloane Associates. And finally, for being much more than booksellers, I am happy to acknowledge my gratitude to Bertram Rota Ltd.; The Gotham Book Mart; House of Books Ltd.; Librairie Tschann; Phoenix Book Shop; and Henry W. Wenning.

GEORGE J. FIRMAGE

New York City
January, 1960

A

Books and Pamphlets by E. E. Cummings

NOTE: Later this year Faber and Faber Ltd., London, will publish *Selected Poems 1923–1958*. Bibliographical details were not available at the time this volume went to press.

A

Books and Pamphlets by E. E. Cummings

A1   EIGHT HARVARD POETS   1917

First edition:

EIGHT HARVARD POETS | E. ESTLIN CUMMINGS | S. FOS-
TER DAMON | J. R. DOS PASSOS | ROBERT HILLYER |
R. S. MITCHELL | WILLIAM A NORRIS | DUDLEY POORE |
CUTHBERT WRIGHT | [*ornament*] | NEW YORK | LAURENCE
J. GOMME | 1917

1 blank leaf, 4 leaves, 3–118 pp., 1 blank leaf. $5\frac{1}{8} \times 7\frac{1}{2}$ inches. $1.00.
Sage green paper over boards, polished gray cloth back, stamped
in maroon on front cover and spine; end papers.

500 copies published in August 1917. The number of copies published and the publication date are based on the detailed account
of the book's publication given by Charles Norman in *The Magic
Maker* (New York: The Macmillan Company, 1958), pp. 56–71.

Contains (pp. 3–10) eight poems by Cummings: 'Thou in whose
sword-great story shine the deeds'*—A CHORUS GIRL ('When thou
hast taken thy last applause, and when'*)—'This is the garden:
colors come and go,'*—'It may not always be so; and I say'*—CREPUS-
CULE ('I will wade out/ till my thighs are steeped in burn-'*)—
FINIS ('Over silent waters/ day descending/ night ascending')—THE
LOVER SPEAKS ('Your little voice/ Over the wires came leaping'*)—
EPITAPH ('Tumbling-hair/ picker of buttercups/ violets').

* Reprinted as 'Thou in whose swordgreat story shine the deeds', 'when
thou hast taken thy last applause, and when', 'this is the garden: colours come
and go,', 'it may not always be so; and i say', 'i will wade out/ till my thighs
are steeped in burning flowers', 'your little voice/ Over the wires came leaping'.

E. E. Cummings

A2   THE ENORMOUS ROOM   (1922)

a. First edition:

THE | ENORMOUS ROOM | BY | E. E. CUMMINGS | [*publisher's device*] BONI <u>AND</u> LIVERIGHT | *Publishers : New York*

2 leaves, vii, 9-271 pp. $5\frac{1}{4} \times 7\frac{7}{8}$ inches. $2.00. Tan cloth stamped in black on front cover and spine; end papers. Light gray-blue dust wrapper printed in royal blue and red (sketch by Cummings on front).

    Published on April 27, 1922. Second and Third printings are noted on the verso of the title page.

    The first edition exists in two states: (1) without the deletion of the fifth word in the last line of page 219; (2) with the word deleted. For a full account of the history and publication of this edition see Charles Norman's *The Magic Maker*, pp. 108-127.

    Contents: Introduction (by Edward Cummings)—I. I Begin a Pilgrimage—II. En Route—III. A Pilgrim's Progress—IV. Le Nouveau—V. A Group of Portraits—VI. Apollyon—VII. An Approach to the Delectable Mountains—VIII. The Wanderer—IX. Zoo-Loo—X. Surplice—XI. Jean Le Nègre—XII. Three Wise Men—XIII. I Say Good-Bye to La Misère.

*b. First English edition ([*1928*]):*

THE | ENORMOUS ROOM | By | E. E. CUMMINGS | With an | Introduction | by | ROBERT GRAVES | [*publisher's device*] | JONATHAN CAPE 30 BEDFORD SQUARE | LONDON

332 pp., 2 blank leaves. $5\frac{1}{4} \times 7\frac{15}{16}$ inches. Deep plum cloth, with fine black thread in cross weave, stamped in gold on spine and in blind on back cover; end papers.

    On verso of title page: FIRST PUBLISHED MCMXXVIII . . .

    The addition of Robert Graves' "Introduction" and the retitling of Edward Cummings' "Introduction", now the "Foreword", are the only outward changes in the contents of the first American edition to be noted in the first English. However, the text, according to Graves, is based on "Cummings' original manuscript" and "contains a good deal of material that does not appear in the American edition, including five or six Portraits in Chapter V, and corrects a very large number of misprints that do."

4

A : Books

c. "Life & Letters" edition ([*1930*]):

THE LIFE AND LETTERS SERIES NO. 2 | [*rule*] | E. E. CUM-
MINGS | THE | ENORMOUS ROOM | With an Introduction
by | ROBERT GRAVES | London — JONATHAN CAPE —
Toronto

> 332 pp., front. (photographic portrait of Cummings by Bachrach).
> $5\frac{1}{4} \times 7\frac{13}{16}$ inches. 4s. 1d. Sage green cloth stamped in silver on front
> cover and spine; end papers. White dust wrapper printed in green.
>
> *On verso of title page:* First published 1928 Reprinted (twice) 1928
> Reissued in The Life & Letters Series 1930
>
> A reprint of the first English edition text.

d. "Travellers' Library" edition ([*1930*]):

THE ENORMOUS ROOM | by | E. E. CUMMINGS | [*pub-
lisher's device*] | NEW YORK | JONATHAN CAPE AND
HARRISON SMITH

> xii, 286 pp., 1 blank leaf. $4\frac{5}{8} \times 6\frac{11}{16}$ inches. $1.00. Blue cloth stamped
> in blind on front cover and in gold on spine; end papers. Tan dust
> wrapper printed in black.
>
> *On verso of title page:* PUBLISHED BY JONATHAN CAPE AND
> HARRISON SMITH, 1930
>
> A reprint, with a few corrections and changes, of the first Ameri-
> can edition.

e. "Modern Library" edition ([*1934*]):

[*Within a thick outer and thin inner ruled rectangular border:*] THE |
ENORMOUS ROOM | [*rule*] | BY | E. E. CUMMINGS | [*rule*]
| WITH A NEW INTRODUCTION BY | THE AUTHOR | [*rule*]
[*publisher's device*] | [*rule*] | BENNETT A. CERF · DONALD
S. KLOPFER | THE MODERN LIBRARY | NEW YORK

> 1 leaf, xviii, 332 pp. $4\frac{1}{4} \times 6\frac{1}{2}$ inches. 95 cents. Brick red cloth stamped
> in gold on front cover and spine; top edge stained plum; end papers
> printed in ochre. White dust wrapper printed in black and green.
>
> 5000 copies published on January 25, 1934.
>
> *On verso of title page:* . . . *First Modern Library Edition* 1934 . . .
>
> Cummings' "Introduction", his father's "Foreword" and the
> restoration, under the direct supervision of the author, of the original
> manuscript text makes the "Modern Library" edition, no. 214 in
> the current series, the most authoritative edition issued to date.

E. E. Cummings

a. First edition:

Tulips and | Chimneys | By E. E. Cummings | THOMAS SELT-ZER | NEW YORK MCMXXIII

125 pp., 1 blank leaf. 6¼ × 8¼ inches. $2.00. Dark purple paper over boards, unbleached linen back, with white paper label printed in purple on spine; flat spine; end papers; top edges stained purple. White dust wrapper printed in black and red.

Published on October 25, 1923. Second printing noted on verso of title page.

The manuscript of *Tulips and Chimneys*, as submitted for publication, contained 139 poems; the book, as published by Thomas Seltzer, sixty-six. To date, no records have been uncovered to indicate who was responsible for the change. The poems omitted in the first edition were eventually published in *&*, *XLI Poems* and *Is 5*. However, the publication, in 1937, of the Archetype edition (see b. and c. below) restored the original manuscript number and arrangement of the poems.

Contents: TULIPS: EPITHALAMION ('Thou aged unreluctant earth who dost')—OF NICOLETTE ('dreaming in marble all the castle lay')—SONGS (I. '(thee will i praise between those rivers whose'—II. 'Always before your voice my soul'—III. 'Thy fingers make early flowers of'—IV. 'All in green went my love riding'—V. 'Doll's boy 's asleep'—VI. 'when god lets my body be')—PUELLA MEA ('Harun Omar and Master Hafiz')—CHANSONS INNOCENTES (I. 'in Just-'—II. 'hist   whist'—III. 'Tumbling-hair/ picker of butter-cups/ violets')—ORIENTALE (I. 'i spoke to thee'—II. 'lean candles hunger in'—III. 'my love'—IV. 'listen// beloved'—V. 'unto thee i'—VI. 'the emperor')—AMORES (I. 'consider O'—II. 'there is a'—III. 'as is the sea marvelous'—IV. 'if i believe'—V. 'the glory is fallen out of'—VI. 'i like'—VII. 'O Distinct'—VIII. 'your little voice/ Over the wires came leaping')—LA GUERRE (I. 'the bigness of cannon'—II. 'O sweet spontaneous')—IMPRESSIONS (I. 'the sky a silver'—II. 'writhe and'—III. 'i was considering how'—IV. 'the hours rise up putting off stars and it is'—V. 'stinging')—PORTRAITS (I. 'the'—II. 'of evident invisibles'—III. 'between nose-red gross' —IV. 'i walked the boulevard'—V. 'the young'—VI. 'but the other'—VII. 'the rose'—VIII. 'Buffalo Bill 's'—IX. 'spring omnipotent goddess thou dost'—X. 'somebody knew Lincoln somebody Xerxes')—POST IMPRESSIONS ('I. 'beyond the brittle towns

asleep'—II. 'the moon is hiding in'—III. 'into the strenuous briefness'—IV. 'i am going to utter a tree, Nobody'—V. 'any man is
wonderful'—VI. 'at the head of this street a gasping organ is
waving moth-'); CHIMNEYS: SONNETS—REALITIES (I. 'the Cambridge
ladies who live in furnished souls'—II. 'goodby Betty, don't remember me'—III. 'ladies and gentlemen this little girl'—IV. 'when
you rang at Dick Mid's Place'—V. '"kitty". sixteen, 5' 1", white,
prostitute.'—VI. 'when thou hast taken by last applause, and
when')—SONNETS—UNREALITIES (I. 'it may not always be so; and
i say'—II. 'god gloats upon Her stunning flesh. Upon'—III. 'it is
at moments after i have dreamed'—IV. 'when citied day with the
sonorous homes'—V. 'a wind has blown the rain away and blown'
—VI. 'a connotation of infinity')—SONNETS—ACTUALITIES (I. 'a
thing most new complete fragile intense,'—II. 'my love is building a building'—III. 'yours is the music for no instrument'—IV.
'by little accurate saints thickly which tread'—V. 'notice the convulsed orange inch of moon').

b. Archetype edition, signed (1937):

[*In green reading up on left:*] TULIPS & CHIMNEYS | [*in black
reading across:*] ARCHETYPE EDITION OF | THE ORIGINAL
MS | 1922 | MOUNT VERNON | THE GOLDEN EAGLE
PRESS | 1937 | [*in green reading down on right:*] BY E·E·CUM-
MINGS

3 blank leaves, 223, [1]pp., 3 blank leaves. 5⅝ × 8 inches. $12.50.
St. Albans' floral decorated paper over boards, sage green polished
cloth back, stamped in gold up and down spine; light green coated
end papers. Boxed.

Colophon (p. [224]): This Archetype Edition of TULIPS AND CHIMNEYS
*is published in two styles, printed on Arnold Unbleached all rag paper.
The first 148 numbered and autographed copies are in deluxe binding. The
remaining 481 numbered copies, of which 333 are for sale in the United States,
are in a special binding. Printed by S. A. Jacobs, The Golden Eagle Press,
Fleetwood, Mount Vernon, New York, U.S.A., in the month of October,
1937. [Number] . . . [signed] E. E. C's*

Published on December 1, 1937.

Contents: TULIPS: EPITHALAMION ('Thou aged unreluctant earth who
dost')—OF NICOLETTE ('dreaming in marble all the castle lay')—
SONGS (I. 'thee will i praise between those rivers whose'—II. 'when
life is quite through with'—III. 'Always before your voice my soul'
—IV. 'Thy fingers make early flowers of'—V. 'All in green went

E. E. Cummings

fourteenth'—VI. 'when you rang at Dick Mid's Place'—VII. 'a fragrant sag of fruit distinctly grouped.'—VIII. 'irreproachable ladies firmly lewd'—IX. 'nearer:breath of my breath:take not thy tingling'—X. '"kitty".   sixteen, 5′ 1″, white, prostitute.'— XI. 'god pity me whom(god distinctly has)'—XII. 'when thou hast taken thy last applause, and when'—XIII. 'it started when Bill's chip let on to'—XIV. 'she sits dropping on a caret of clenched arms'—XV. 'unnoticed woman from whose kind large flesh'— XVI. 'twentyseven bums give a prostitute the once'—XVII. 'of this wilting wall the colour drub'—XVIII. 'whereas by dark really released, the modern'—XIX. 'my girl's tall with hard long eyes'— XX. 'Dick Mid's large bluish face without eyebrows'—XXI. 'life boosts herself rapidly at me')—SONNETS—UNREALITIES (I. 'and what were roses. Perfume? for i do'—II. 'when unto nights of autumn do complain'—III. 'it may not always be so; and i say'— IV. 'Thou in whose swordgreat story shine the deeds'—V. 'when my sensational moments are no more'—VI. 'god gloats upon Her stunning flesh. Upon'—VII. 'it is at moments after i have dreamed' —VIII. 'when the proficient poison of sure sleep'—IX. 'this is the garden: colours come and go,'—X. 'when citied day with the sonorous homes'—XI. 'a wind has blown the rain away and blown' —XII. 'I have seen her a stealthily frail'—XIII. 'when learned darkness from our searched world'—XIV. 'who's most afraid of death? thou/ art of him'—XV. 'come nothing to my comparable soul'—XVI. 'a connotation of infinity'—XVII. 'will suddenly trees leap from winter and will')—SONNETS—ACTUALITIES (I. 'when my love comes to see me it's'—II. 'it is funny, you will be dead some day.'—III. 'i have loved, let us see if that's all.'—IV. 'a thing most new complete fragile intense,'—V. 'even a pencil has fear to'— VI. 'let's live suddenly without thinking'—VII. 'my love is building a building'—VIII. 'fabulous against   ,a,fathoming jelly'— IX. 'yours is the music for no instrument'—X. 'by little accurate saints thickly which tread'—XI. 'autumn is: that between there and here'—XII. 'notice the convulsed orange inch of moon'— XIII. 'O Thou to whom the musical white spring'—XIV. 'the ivory performing rose'—XV. 'my naked lady framed'—XVI. 'i have found what you are like'—XVII. 'G O N splashes-sink'— XVIII. 'my sonnet is A light goes on in'—XIX. '(the phonograph's voice like a keen spider skipping'—XX. 'perhaps it is to feel strike' —XXI. 'let us tremble)a personal radiance sits'—XXII. 'utterly and amusingly i am pash'—XXIV. [*sic*] 'and this day it was Spring . . . . us').

E. E. Cummings

c. Archetype edition, unsigned:

$7.50. Sage green paper over boards, vellum back stamped in green
up and down spine. Cream dust wrapper printed in black and green.
Colophon as above, but unsigned.
Published on December 1, 1937.

A4   AND   1925

a. First edition, Vidalon hand-made paper issue:

&° | by | E. E. Cummings | New York | PRIVATELY PRINTED
| 1925

2 blank leaves, 116 pp., 1 blank leaf. $5\frac{1}{2} \times 8\frac{3}{8}$ inches. Gold specked
green paper over boards printed in red on front cover and spine.

Colophon (p. [2]): THIS EDITION CONSISTS OF 111 COPIES ON VIDALON
HAND-MADE PAPER, AND 222 COPIES ON DE COVERLY RAG LAID NUM-
BERED I TO 333 OF WHICH THIS COPY IS NUMBER . . . *(signed)* E. E. C's
Published on February 14, 1925.

Contents: A: POST IMPRESSIONS (I. 'windows go orange in the slowly.'
—II. 'riverly is a flower'—III. 'the wind is a Lady with'—IV. 'Take
for example this:'—V. 'Paris; this April sunset completely utters'—
VI. 'I remark this beach has been used too.   much Too.'—
VII. 'my smallheaded pearshaped'—VIII. 'i was sitting in
mcsorley's.   outside it was New'—IX. 'of this sunset(which is
so'—X. 'SNO'—XI. 'my eyes are fond of the east side'—XII. 'suppose'—XIII. 'the dress was a suspicious madder, importing the
cruelty of roses.'—XIV. 'inthe,exquisite;')—PORTRAITS (I. 'being'
—II. 'Babylon slim'—III. 'ta'—IV. 'the waddling'—V. 'raise the
shade'—VI. 'Cleopatra built'—VII. 'between the breasts'—
VIII. 'when the spent day begins to frail'—IX. 'impossibly'—
X. 'here is little Effie's head'—XI. 'her'—XII. 'little ladies
more'); N: &: SEVEN POEMS (I. 'i will be'—II. 'i'll tell you a dream
i had once i was away up in the'—III. 'Spring is like a perhaps
hand'—IV. 'Who/ threw the silver dollar up into the tree?/ I
didn't'—V. 'gee i like to think of dead it means nearer because
deeper'—VI. '(one!)'—VII. 'who knows if the moon's'); D: SON-
NETS—REALITIES (I. 'O It's Nice To Get Up In,the slipshod mucous
kiss'—II. 'my strength becoming wistful in a glib'—III. 'the dirty
colours of her kiss have just'—IV. 'light cursed falling in a singular
block'—V. 'the bed is not very big'—VI. 'the poem her belly
marched through me as'— VII. 'an amiable putrescence carpen-

ters'—VIII. 'her careful distinct sex whose sharp lips comb'—
IX. 'irreproachable ladies firmly lewd'—X. 'nearer:breath of my
breath:take not thy tingling'—XI. 'god pity me whom(god distinctly has)'—XII. 'even a pencil has fear to'—XIII. 'unnoticed
woman from whose kind large flesh'—XIV. 'she sits dropping on
a caret of clenched arms'—XV. 'of this wilting wall the colour
drub'—XVI. 'it started when Bill's chip let on to'—XVII. 'whereas
by dark really released, the modern'—XVIII. 'my girl's tall with
hard long eyes'—XIX. 'in making Marjorie god hurried' —
XX. 'Dick Mid's large bluish face without eyebrows'—
XXI. 'twentyseven bums give a prostitute the once'—XXII. 'life
boosts herself rapidly at me')—SONNETS—ACTUALITIES (I. 'when my
love comes to see me it's'—II. 'it is funny, you will be dead some
day.'—III. 'i have loved, let us see if that's all.'—IV. 'utterly and
amusingly i am pash'—V. 'before the fragile gradual throne of
night'—VI. 'when i have thought of you somewhat too'—VII. 'autumn is: that between there and here'—VIII. 'fabulous against
,a,fathoming jelly'—IX. 'let's live suddenly without thinking'—
X. 'if i should sleep with a lady called death'—XI. 'my naked lady
framed'—XII. 'i have found what you are like'—XIII. 'upon
the room's/ silence, i will sew'—XIV. 'the ivory performing rose'—
XV. '(the phonograph's voice like a keen spider skipping'—
XVI. 'a blue woman with sticking out breasts hanging'—XVII. 'let
us tremble)a personal radiance sits'—XVIII. '—G O N splashes-
sink'—XIX. 'the mind is its own beautiful prisoner.'—XX. 'my
sonnet is A light goes on in'—XXI. 'when you went away it was
morning'—XXII. 'you asked me to come: it was raining a little,'—
XXIII. 'and this day it was Spring . . . . us'—XXIV. 'i like my
body when it is with your').

b. First edition, De Coverly rag laid paper issue:

Except for the paper, this issue is exactly like the one on Vidalon
hand-made paper.

A5   XLI POEMS   1925

First edition:

XLI POEMS | BY E. E. CUMMINGS | NEW YORK | THE
DIAL PRESS | MCMXXV

2 blank leaves, 3 leaves, 1 blank leaf, 9–54 pp., 3 blank leaves. $5\frac{1}{2} \times 8\frac{1}{4}$
inches. $2.50. Blue cloth with gold paper label printed in black on
front cover; end papers.

E. E. Cummings

Published on April 11, 1925

Contents: SONGS (I. 'the/ sky/ was'—II. 'of my'—III. 'when life is quite through with'—IV. 'into the smiting'—V. 'Where's Madge then,'—VI. 'after five'—VII. 'between green/ mountains'—VIII. 'in the rain-'—IX. 'Lady of Silence'—X. 'the hills'— XI. 'i will wade out/ till my thighs are steeped in burning flowers'—XII. 'cruelly, love')—CHANSONS INNOCENTES (I. 'why did you go'—II. 'little tree')—PORTRAITS (I. 'conversation with my friend is particularly'—II. 'one April dusk the'—III. 'Picasso'—IV. 'the skinny voice'—V. 'as usual i did not find him in cafes, the more dissolute'—VI. 'it's just like a coffin's'—VII. 'my mind is'—VIII. '5'—IX. 'at the ferocious phenomenon of 5 o'clock i find myself')—LA GUERRE (I. 'earth like a tipsy'—II. 'Humanity i love you')—SONNETS (I. 'when learned darkness from our searched world'*—II. 'O Thou to whom the musical white spring'—III. 'when unto nights of autumn do complain'—IV. 'this is the garden: colours come and go,'—V. 'Thou in whose swordgreat story shine the deeds'—VI. 'when the proficient poison of sure sleep'—VII. 'and what were roses. Perfume? for i do'—VIII. 'come nothing to my comparable soul'—IX. 'when my sensational moments are no more'—X. 'I have seen her a stealthily frail'—XI. 'who's most afraid of death? thou/ art of him'—XII. 'perhaps it is to feel strike'—XIII. 'when i am in Boston, i do not speak.'—XIV. 'will suddenly trees leap from winter and will'—XV. 'a fragrant sag of fruit distinctly grouped.'—XVI. 'by god i want above fourteenth').

* Reprinted as 'if learned darkness from our searched world'.

A6   IS 5   1926

a. First edition, ordinary issue:

[*In black:*] by E. E. Cummings | [*rule*] | is | [*in red:*] 5 | [*in black:*] NEW YORK | BONI & LIVERIGHT | 1926

6 leaves, 3–115 pp. $5\frac{1}{2} \times 8\frac{1}{4}$ inches. $2.50. Gold specked orange paper over boards, black cloth back, stamped in black on front cover and in gold on spine; end papers. Cream dust wrapper printed in black and red.

Published on June 14, 1926. *On verso of first leaf (first edition only):* OF THIS BOOK there is also a special limited edition consisting of seventy-seven copies on special paper specially bound numbered and

A : Books

autographed of which seventy copies are for sale   Second and third
printings are noted on the verso of the title page.

Contents: Foreword—One: I. FIVE AMERICANS (I. LIZ ('with breathing as (faithfully) her lownecked')—II. MAME ('she puts down the
handmirror. "Look at" arranging')—III. GERT ('joggle i think
will do it although the glad')—IV. MARJ ('"life?/ Listen" the
feline she with radishred')—V. FRAN ('should i entirely ask of god
why'))—II. POEM, OR BEAUTY HURTS MR. VINAL ('take it from me
kiddo')—III. 'curtains part)'—IV. 'workingman with hand so
hairy-sturdy'—V. 'yonder deadfromtheneckup graduate of a'—
VI. 'Jimmie's got a goil/ goil/ goil,/ Jimmie'—VII. 'the waddling'
—VIII. 'listen my children and you'—IX. 'even if all desires things
moments be'—X. 'death is more than'—XI. 'nobody loses all the
time'—XII. 'now dis "daughter" uv eve(who aint precisely
slim)sim'—XIII. '(and i imagine'—XIV. 'it really must'—
XV. ITEM ('this man is o so')—XVI. 'it started when Bill's chip
let on to'—XVII. 'IKEY(GOLDBERG)'S WORTH I'M'—
XVIII. ? ('why are these pipples taking their hets off?')—XIX. 'this
young question mark man'—XX. 'mr youse needn't be so spry'
—XXI. 'i was sitting in mcsorley's. outside it was New'—
XXII. 'she being Brand'—XXIII. 'slightly before the middle of
Congressman Pudd'—XXIV. 'Dick Mid's large bluish face with-
out eyebrows'—XXV. ODE ('o// the sweet & aged people')—
XXVI. 'on the Madam's best april the'—XXVII. '(as that named
Fred'—XXVIII. 'my uncle'—XXIX. 'than(by yon sunset's wintry
glow'—XXX. 'weazened Irrefutable unastonished'—XXXI. MEM-
ORABILIA ('stop look &')—XXXII. 'a man who had fallen among
thieves'—XXXIII. 'Babylon slim'—XXXIV. 'this evangelist'—
XXXV. '(ponder,darling,these busted statues'—XXXVI. 'ta'—
XXXVII. 'poets yeggs and thirsties'—XXXVIII. 'Will i ever
forget that precarious moment?'—XXXIX. 'voices to voices, lip
to lip'—XL. 'life hurl my'; Two: I. 'the season' tis, my lovely
lambs,'—II. 'opening of the chambers close'—III. '"next to of
course god america i'—IV. 'it's jolly'—V. 'look at this)'—
VI. 'first Jock he'—VII. 'lis'—VIII. 'come, gaze with me upon
this dome'—IX. 'little ladies more'—X. '16 heures'—XI. 'my sweet
old etcetera'; THREE: I. 'now that fierce few'—II. 'Among/ these/
red pieces of '—III. 'it is winter a moon in the afternoon'—IV. 'impossibly'—V. 'inthe,exquisite;'—VI. 'candles and'—VII. 'Paris;
this April sunset completely utters'—VIII. 'will out of the kindness
of their hearts a few philosophers tell me'—IX. 'but observe;
although'—X. 'sunlight was over'; FOUR: I. 'the moon looked into

my window'—II. 'if being morticed with a dream'*—III. 'here's a
little mouse)and'—IV. 'but if i should say'—V. 'in spite of everything'—VI. 'you are not going to, dear. You are not going to and'—
VII. 'since feeling is first'—VIII. 'some ask praise of their fellows'—
IX. 'supposing i dreamed this)'—X. 'you are like the snow only'
—XI. 'because/ you go away i give roses who'—XII. 'you being in
love'—XIII. 'Nobody wears a yellow'—XIV. 'it is so long since
my heart has been with yours'—XV. 'i am a beggar always'—
XVI. 'if within tonight's erect'—XVII. 'how this uncouth enchanted'—XVIII. 'i go to this window'; FIVE: I. 'after all white
horses are in bed'—II. 'touching you i say (it being Spring'—
III. 'along the brittle treacherous bright streets'—IV. 'our touching
hearts slenderly comprehend'—V. 'if i have made, my lady, intricate'.

* Reprinted as 'if being mortised with a dream'.

b. *Limited issue:*

5½ × 8 5/16 inches. $7.50. Gold specked black paper over boards, black
cloth back, stamped in gold on spine; end papers. Gold specked black
paper covered slip case with black paper label printed in gold on side.
   Colophon (*verso of first leaf*)*:* OF THIS EDITION there have been printed
SEVENTY-SEVEN copies on special paper specially bound numbered
and autographed of which seventy copies are for sale   THIS IS COPY
NUMBER . . . [*signed*] E. E. C's
   Published on June 14, 1926.

A7   HIM   1927

a. *First edition, ordinary issue:*

[*In black:*] by e e cummings | [*rule*] | [*in red:*] HIM | [*in black:
rule*] | looking forward into the past or looking | backward
into the future I | walk on the highest | hill and | I laugh | about
| it | all | the way | ANNE BARTON | [*ornament*] | NEW YORK
| *Boni & Liveright* | 1927

   2 blank leaves, 3 leaves, 3–145 pp., 3 blank leaves. 5½ × 8 inches.
$2.50. White paper over boards, black cloth back, stamped in black
on front cover (line drawing within a ruled border signed, in mirror
image, "E. E. C's") and red on spine; end papers.   White dust
wrapper printed in black and red ("AN IMAGINARY DIALOGUE

A : Books

BETWEEN AN AUTHOR AND A PUBLIC *As Imagined by* E. E. CUMMINGS" printed on front flap).

Published on November 1, 1927. *On verso of first leaf (first edition only):* OF THIS BOOK ¶THERE *is also a special limited edition of* 160 *numbered and signed copies of which* 150 *are for sale.*

b. Limited issue:

5⅝ × 8⅜ inches. $10.00. Black paper over boards, vellum back and corners, stamped in gold on front cover (same design as ordinary issue) and black on spine; end papers. Black paper covered slip case with white paper label printed in black and red (same design as front of ordinary issue dust wrapper) on side.

Colophon (verso of first leaf): CERTIFICATE ¶*This edition is limited to* 160 *numbered and signed copies, of which* 150 *copies are for sale.* THIS COPY IS NUMBER . . . *[signed]* E. E. C's

Published on November 1, 1927.

A8   CHRISTMAS TREE   [1928]

First edition:

[*In orange: seven stars and a crescent moon*] | [*in green reading up:*] Christmas tree | [*in green and orange: vertical ornamental rule*] | [*in green reading down:*] by e e cummingS | [*the complete title enclosed in a green ruled border lined with orange*] [New York: The American Book Bindery, Inc.]

1 blank leaf, [11], [1] pp., 1 blank leaf. front.(silver page). All leaves are double fold (top edge uncut) with text of poem printed in green parallel to the spine within a green ruled border. 5⅛ × 7⅝ inches. Silver specked green paper over boards, red cloth back, with silver paper label printed in red at head of red cloth on front cover; flat spine; light green coated end papers.

Colophon (p. [12]): XMAS TREE BY E E CUMMINGS HERE PRINTED BY PERMISSION TYPOGRAPHY BY S. A. JACOBS THE WHOLE MADE INTO A BOOK IN NEW YORK IN THIS YEAR OF GRACE MCMXXVIII BY THE AMERICAN BOOK BINDERY INC

Published in December (?) 1928. Several copies examined, though not all, bore the following notice on the verso of the title page: PRINTED FOR NATIONAL CHROMIUM CORPORATION

This is the first separate publication of 'little tree'. It was first published in book form in *XLI Poems*.

E. E. Cummings

A9 [NO TITLE] 1930

First edition:

[*In black on a yellow rectangular ground:*] BY | E. E. CUMMINGS | WITH ILLUSTRATIONS | BY THE AUTHOR | NEW YORK MDCCCCXXX | COVICI FRIEDE PUBLISHERS

vi, 2 leaves, [11]–63, [1] pp., incl. front. (yellow rectangle) and 8 illus. (line drawings in black on a yellow rectangular ground). 9¼ × 12¼ inches. $7.50. Light gray cloth stamped in silver on front cover and in blind down spine; flat spine; end papers.

Colophon (*p.* [64]): THIS EDITION IS LIMITED TO 491 COPIES EACH SIGNED BY THE AUTHOR THIS IS NUMBER . . . [*signed*] E. E. C's

Published on September 26, 1930.

Contents: An Imaginary Dialogue between ALMOST Any Publisher And A *certain* Author A.D. 1930—THE GARDEN OF EDEN . . . *before the dawn of history* . . .*—CHAPTER I—THE DEATH OF ABRAHAM LINCOLN . . . *even prominent people* . . . —CHAPTER II—THE SWAN AND LEDA . . . *protect your dear ones* . . . —CHAPTER III—THE FRIEND IN NEED. . . *a boon to travellers* . . . —CHAPTER IV—THE SPINSTER'S DILEMMA . . . *but a parrot did* . . . —CHAPTER V—THE HELPING HAND . . . *nobody is exempt* . . . —CHAPTER VI—THE FIRST ROBIN . . . *if the punishment fitted the crime* . . . —CHAPTER VII—THE DOG IN THE MANGER . . . *Aesop knew* . . . —CHAPTER VIII.

* Titles preceding chapter numbers are illustrations.

A10 CIOPW 1931

First edition:

[*The author's signature in red, blue or green watercolor:*] C's | [*in black:*] C I O P W | Published by Covici=Friede in Mdccccxxxi in the City of New York

119pp. incl. plates. 9⅜ × 12¼ inches. $20.00. Linen weave cloth stamped in silver on front cover; end papers. Glassine dust wrapper.

Colophon (*p.* [2]): THIS EDITION IS LIMITED TO 391 COPIES EACH SIGNED BY THE AUTHOR ON TITLE PAGE THIS COPY IS NUMBER . . .

Published on January 26, 1931.

Contents: [Foreword]; CHARCOAL: asleep—asleep—awake—bois de Boulogne—Larionov dessine; INK: Calchidas—Central Park—Chaplin—dancers—elephant—Funchal—gonzesse—l'amour—landscape—

lovin—Shargel—train; OIL COLORS: acrobats—African queen—bath-
ers—Chocorua—course—elephant—girl in grey—Greb-Flowers—
Harlem—letter—merrygoround—New Hampshire, winter—New
York, 1927—noise number 13—nude—nude—nude—nude—nude—
pipe—portrait: Anne Barton—portrait: Diana Barton—portrait:
eyes—portrait: face—portrait: hair—portrait: head—portrait: Joe
Gould—portrait: M. R. Werner—portrait: self—portrait: self—road
—Roscoff—Seine—Seine—Small's—Spanish dancer—still life—still
life—still life—still life—storm—straw-hat nigger—street—Sugar
Cane—suicide—sundown—train; PENCIL: Dial-G.S.—Dial-S.T.—
Dial-S.W.—Faial—Goliath—Nederlands—nude—Wien—Y.x,; WA-
TERCOLORS: boulevard Montmartre—Chocorua: sunset—danseuse
"egyptienne"—day—dockhand—girl reading—interior—jardins des
Tuileries—Joy farm—l'heure du thé—marée basse—marée haute—
moonrise—Napoli—nymph—Pornic—porte Saint Denis—portrait—
Saint James—shimmy—Silver lake—sombra (Sevilla)—sunset.

AII   VIVA   1931

a. First edition, ordinary issue:

[*In black:*] E. E. CUMMINGS | [*in white on a gray square ground:*]
W | [*in black:*] HORACE LIVERIGHT INC | PUBLISHERS ·
NEW YORK · MCMXXXI [*all enclosed in a gray ruled border*]

2 blank leaves, 1 leaf, 1 blank leaf, [70]pp., 1 blank leaf. 7 × 11$\frac{7}{8}$
inches. $2.50. Cream paper over boards, monk's cloth back, stamped
in brown on spine; flat spine; end papers. Silver coated dust wrapper
printed in black.

Published on October 16, 1931.

Contents: I. ',mean-'—II. 'oil tel duh woil doi sez'—III. 'the
surely'—IIII. 'there are 6 doors.'—V. 'myself,walking in Dragon
st'—VI. 'but mr can you maybe listen there's'—VII. 'Space being
(don't forget to remember)Curved'—VIII. '(one fine day)'—
VIIII. 'y is a WELL KNOWN ATHLETE'S BRIDE'—X. 'thethe'—
XI. 'a/mong crum/bling people(a'—XII. 'poor But TerFLY'
—XIII. 'remarked Robinson Jefferson'—XIIII. 'what time is it i
wonder never mind'—XV. 'well)here's looking at ourselves'—
XVI. 'tell me not how electricity or'—XVII. 'FULL SPEED
ASTERN)'—XVIII. '"Gay" is the captivating cognomen of a Young
Woman of cambridge, mass.'—XVIIII. 'i will cultivate within'—
XX. 'but granted that it's nothing paradoxically enough beyond

E. E. Cummings

mere personal'—XXI. 'helves surling out of eakspeasies per(reel) hapsingly'—XXII. 'Lord John Unalive(having a fortune of fifteen-grand'—XXIII. 'buncha hardboil guys frum duh A.C. fulla'—XXIIII. 'from the cognoscenti'—XXV. 'ohld song'—XXVI. 'murderfully in midmost o.c.an'—XXVII. 'the first president to be loved by his'—XXVIII. 'serene immediate silliest and whose'—XXVIIII. 'in a middle of a room'—XXX. 'i sing of Olaf glad and big'—XXXI. 'memory believes'—XXXII. 'Wing Wong,uninterred at twice'—XXXIII. 'innerly'—XXXIIII. 'don't cries to please my'—XXXV. 'what is strictly fiercely and wholly dies'—XXXVI. 'sunset)edges become swiftly'—XXXVII. 'how// ses humble.'—XXXVIII. 'n(o)w/ the'—XXXVIIII. 'An(fragrance) Of'—XL. 'thou/firsting a hugeness of twi/-light'—XLI. 'twi-/is-Light bird'—XLII. 'structure,miraculous challenge,devout am'—XLIII. 'if there are any heavens my mother will(all by herself)have'—XLIIII. 'i'd think "wonder'—XLV. 'you'—XLVI. 'i met a man under the moon'—XLVII. 'when rain whom fear'—XLVIII. 'come a little further—why be afraid—'—XLVIIII. 'a light Out)/ & first of all foam'—L. 'when hair falls off and eyes blur And'—LI. 'a clown's smirk in the skull of a baboon'—LII. 'it)It will it'—LIII. 'breathe with me this fear'—LIIII. 'if i love You'—LV. 'speaking of love(of'—LVI. 'lady will you come with me into'—LVII. 'somewhere i have never travelled,gladly beyond'—LVIII. 'is there a flower(whom'—LVIIII. 'my darling since'—LX. 'because i love you)last night'—LXI. 'if you and i awakening'—LXII. 'item:is/ Clumsily with of'—LXIII. 'be unto love as rain is unto colour;create'—LXIIII. 'granted the all/ saving our young kiss only'—LXV. 'but being not amazing:without love'—LXVI. 'nothing is more exactly terrible than'—LXVII. 'put off your faces,Death:for day is over'—LXVIII. 'but if a living dance upon dead minds'—LXVIIII. 'so standing,our eyes filled with wind,and the'—LXX. 'here is the ocean,this is moonlight:say'.

b. *Limited issue:*

1 blank leaf, 2 leaves, 1 blank leaf, [70]pp., 1 blank leaf. $7\frac{1}{8} \times 12$ inches. $7.50. Light gray paper over boards, silver sheen cloth back, stamped in silver on spine; flat spine; end papers. Glassine dust wrapper. Black paper covered slip case with silver label printed in black on side.

Colophon (verso of first leaf): OF THIS FIRST EDITION of this book of poems by E. E. Cummings there have been made ninety-five

copies on special paper and individually bound of which eighty-five will be for sale. THIS IS COPY NUMBER . . . [*signed*] E. E. C's
Published on October 16, 1931.

A12   THE RED FRONT   [1933]

First edition:

Louis Aragon | THE RED FRONT | Translated by | E. E. CUM-MINGS | CONTEMPO PUBLISHERS | Chapel Hill, North Carolina

1 blank leaf, [10]pp. $6\frac{7}{8} \times 9\frac{13}{16}$ inches. Red paper wrappers printed in black on front cover; stapled.
Approximately 200 copies published on March 22, 1933.

A13   EIMI   [1933]

a. First edition:

∈ Ǝ | CUMMINGS | EIMI [*Facing page.* NEW YORK, COVICI, FRIEDE, PUBLISHERS, MDCCCCXXXIII]

2 leaves, 3–432pp., 1 leaf, 2 blank leaves. $6\frac{1}{2} \times 8\frac{1}{2}$ inches. $3.00. Yellow cloth stamped in black on front cover and spine; end papers. Cream dust wrapper printed in black.
Colophon (verso of last leaf): Covici, Friede, Inc., publishers of EIMI, announce that this, the first edition, printed from type, has been limited to 1381 copies; representing the number of orders received by them up to February 15, 1933 The author joins with the publishers in congratulating S. A. Jacobs; who designed the format of EIMI, solved all technical problems connected with the typesetting and printing, and from start to finish personally supervised the book's production [number] . . . [*signed*] E. E. C's
Published on March 28, 1933. Second printing, with only the acknowledgment to Jacobs on the verso of the last leaf, noted on verso of first leaf.

b. Second edition ([1949]):

E. E. CUMMINGS | [*rule*] | EIMI | [*rule*] | WILLIAM SLOANE ASSOCIATES, INC. | *Publishers New York*

4 leaves, 3–432pp. $5\frac{1}{2} \times 8\frac{7}{16}$ inches. $5.00. Yellow cloth stamped in red on front cover and spine; end papers; top edges stained red. White dust wrapper printed in yellow, black and red.

1500 copies published in February (?) 1949.

Twenty-seven hundred sets of sheets were printed for this edition of *Eimi* from plates that were photolithographed from the first edition. The unbound sheets were later remaindered and bound in a loosely woven unpolished yellow cloth printed in reddish brown on the front cover and spine. The top edges of the remaindered copies are unstained.

c. Third edition, paperbound issue ([1958]):

E. E. CUMMINGS | [*rule*] | EIMI | [*rule*] | GROVE PRESS INC. NEW YORK

1 blank leaf, 4 leaves, xix, 432pp., 1 blank leaf. $5\frac{1}{4} \times 7\frac{13}{16}$ inches. $2.45. White wrapper printed in yellow, black and red; sewn.

3000 copies published on August 25, 1958, as Evergreen Book E-113.

Contains (pp. i-xix) "SKETCH FOR A PREFACE TO THE FOURTH EDITION OF EIMI" by Cummings. The reference to the "fourth" edition is an error; it should read "third".

d. Third edition, clothbound issue:

$5\frac{1}{2} \times 8$ inches. $4.75. Dark gray cloth stamped in gold on front cover and down and across spine; end papers. White dust wrapper printed in black.

1000 copies published on August 25, 1958.

e. Third edition, limited issue:

1 blank leaf, 5 leaves, xix, 432pp., 1 blank leaf. $5\frac{1}{4} \times 8$ inches. $15.00. Beige paper over boards, brown cloth back, stamped in gray and fuchsia on front paper cover and in gold up cloth on front cover and down and across spine; end papers.

Colophon (recto of fourth leaf): This is a SPECIALLY BOUND, LIMITED EDITION of [*in ink*] 26 *Numbered copies, of which this is copy number* [*in ink: letters A–Z*] . . . [*signed*] E. E. C's

Copies of this edition were not ready for distribution until October 1958.

A14   NO THANKS   [1935]

a. First edition, holograph issue:

[*In gold script:*] no thanks [*Page* [2]. . . . Published at New York by The Golden Eagle Press . . .]

A : Books

Cover title, [79], [1]pp. Text printed parallel to the spine except for poem 44 which is in holograph. 7¼ × 5½ inches. $99.00. Full levant morocco—a different color for each copy with variant hand tooled decorations in gold—stamped in gold on cover and across spine; end papers.

Colophon (p.[2]): . . . HOLOGRAPH EDITION *On Inomachi Japanese vellum Limited to nine copies for sale Numbered I–IX Signed* . . . *[number at bottom of page] [signed, p. [80]]* E. E. C's

Published on April 15, 1935.

Contents: 1. 'mOOn Over tOwns mOOn'—2. 'moon over gai'—3. 'that which we who're alive in spite of mirrors'—4. 'a)glazed mind layed in a/ urinal'—5. 'i'.—6. 'exit a kind of unkindness exit'—7. 'sonnet entitled how to run the world)'—8. 'the(/Wistfully'—9. 'o pr'—10. 'little man'—11. 'çi gît 1 Foetus(unborn to not die'—12. 'why why'—13. 'r-p-o-p-h-e-s-s-a-g-r'—14. 'mouse)Won'—15. 'one nonsufficiently inunderstood'—16. 'may i feel said he'—17. 'o// sure)but'—18. 'this little'—19. 'who before dying demands not rebirth'—20. 'go(perpe)go'—21. 'IN)/all those who got'—22. 'when muckers pimps and tratesmen'—23. 'he does not have to feel because he thinks'—24. '"let's start a magazine'—25. 'this(that'—26. 'what does little Ernest croon'—27. 'little joe gould has lost his teeth and doesn't know where'—28. 'that famous fatheads find that each'—29. 'most(people'—30. 'kumrads die because they're told)'—31. 'does yesterday's perfection seem not quite'—32. 'numb(and'—33. 'emptied.hills.listen.'—34. 'snow)says!Says'—35. 'how dark and single,where he ends,the earth'—36. 'into a truly'—37. 'conceive a man,should he have anything'—38. 'SNOW'—39. 'move'—40. 'as if as'—41. 'here's to opening and upward,to leaf and to sap'—42. 'out of a supermetamathical subpreincestures'—43. 'theys sO alive/(who is/?niggers)'—44. *[in holograph]* 'the boys i mean are not refined'—45. 'sometimes/ in)Spring a someone will lie(glued'—46. 'swi(/across!gold's'—47. 'ondumonde"'—48. 'floatfloafloflf'—49. 'silent unday by silently not night'—50. 'much i cannot)'—51. 'at dust/ just when'—52. 'Spring(side'—53. 'what a proud dreamhorse pulling(smoothloomingly)through'—54. 'Jehovah buried,Satan dead,'—55. 'worshipping Same'—56. 'this mind made war'—57. 'when/ from a sidewalk/ out of(blown never quite to'—58. 'love is a place'—59. '(b/eLl/s?/bE'—60. 'sh estiffl'—61. 'love's function is to fabricate unknownness'—62. 'we)under)over,the thing of floating Of'—63. 'birds(/here, inven'—64. 'Do.'—65. 'if night's mostness(and whom did merely day'—66. 'death(having lost)put on his universe'—67. 'come(all you mischief-'—68. 'be of love(a little)'—69. 'reason let others give and realness bring—'—70. 'brIght'—71. 'morsel miraculous and meaningless'.

b. De luxe issue:

[*In red script:*] no thanks [*Page* [2]. .... Published at New York by The Golden Eagle Press . . .]

Page for poem 44 is blank except for poem's number and note reading: "*In holograph edition only*". $12.50. Royal blue cloth stamped in red on cover and across spine; end papers; all edges stained red. Glassine dust wrapper.
Colophon (*p.* [2]): DE LUXE EDITION *On Whitchurch English hand-made paper Limited to ninety copies for sale Numbered 1–90 Signed* . . . [*number at bottom of page*] . . . [*signed, p.* [*80*]] E. E. C's
Published on April 15, 1935.

c. First trade issue:

$7.50. Beige cloth stamped in red on cover and across spine; flat spine; end papers; all edges stained blue. Sand dust wrapper printed in red.
Colophon (*p.* [2]): . . . FIRST TRADE EDITION *On Ricardi Japanese paper Limited to nine hundred copies for sale Not Numbered*
Published on April 15, 1935.

A15   TOM   [1935]

First edition:

TOM | E·E | CUMMINGS [*Page* [2]. ARROW EDITIONS · NEW YORK]

1 blank leaf, 37pp., 2 blank leaves. Col. front. ("TOM" by Ben Shahn). $6\frac{1}{4} \times 8\frac{5}{8}$ inches. $3.00. Brown cloth stamped in silver on front cover and down spine; light brown end papers. Tan dust wrapper printed in rust.
1500 copies published on October 15, 1935.
Cummings "ballet based on 'Uncle Tom's Cabin'" has been scored by David Diamond. To date, Diamond's music has failed to receive either performance or publication.

A : Books

A16   ONE OVER TWENTY   [1936]

First edition:

$\frac{1}{20}$ | *Poems by* | E. E. CUMMINGS | *A Selection made* | *by the*
Author | Roger Roughton | Contemporary Poetry and Prose |
Editions | 1 PARTON STREET, LONDON, W.C.1

1 blank leaf, [27], [1]pp., 1 blank leaf. $5\frac{7}{16} \times 8\frac{1}{2}$ inches. 2s. White
paper boards printed in blue on front cover; sewn.
On verso of title page: First published in December 1936 . . .
   Contents: TULIPS AND CHIMNEYS: 1. 'O sweet spontaneous'—
2. 'Buffalo Bill 's'—3. 'somebody knew Lincoln somebody Xerxes';
XLI POEMS: 4. 'Picasso'—5. 'the skinny voice'—6. 'Humanity i
love you'; &: 7. 'Spring is like a perhaps hand'; Is 5: 8. 'a man
who had fallen among thieves'—9. 'voices to voices, lip to lip'—
10. 'the moon looked into my window'—11. 'here's a little mouse)
and'—12. 'since feeling is first'; VIVA: 13. 'i sing of Olaf glad
and big'—14. 'don't cries to please my'—15. 'come a little further
—why be afraid—'—16. 'but if a living dance upon dead minds';
No THANKS: 17. 'sonnet entitled how to run the world)'—18. 'does
yesterday's perfection seem not quite'—19. 'conceive a man,should
he have anything'—20. 'come(all you mischief-'.

A17   COLLECTED POEMS   [1938]

First edition:

Collected Poems | E. E. Cummings | *Harcourt, Brace and Com-*
pany New York

[328]pp., 2 blank leaves. $5\frac{3}{8} \times 8\frac{7}{16}$ inches. $3.00. Light burnt orange
cloth stamped in black and white on front cover and spine; end
papers. White dust wrapper printed in beige and black.
   1000 copies published on February 24, 1938. *On verso of title page:*
. . . first edition . . .
   Contents: Introduction—TULIPS AND CHIMNEYS: 1. '(thee will i
praise between those rivers whose'—2. 'Thy fingers make early
flowers of'—3. 'Tumbling-hair/ picker of buttercups/ violets'—
4. 'my love'—5. 'it is at moments after i have dreamed'—6. 'All
in green went my love riding'—7. 'god gloats upon Her stunning
flesh. Upon'—8. 'when citied day with the sonorous homes'—
9. 'listen// beloved'—10. 'of evident invisibles'—11. 'Doll's boy
's asleep'—12. 'by little accurate saints thickly which tread'—

13. 'the hours rise up putting off stars and it is'—14. 'beyond the brittle towns asleep'—15. 'Always before your voice my soul'—16. 'when god lets my body be'—17. 'a connotation of infinity'—18. 'the moon is hiding in'—19. 'the glory is fallen out of'—20. 'a wind has blown the rain away and blown'—21. 'O sweet spontaneous'—22. 'but the other'—23. 'any man is wonderful'—24. 'hist whist'—25. 'stinging'—26. 'spring omnipotent goddess thou dost'—27. 'at the head of this street a gasping organ is waving moth-'—28. 'the Cambridge ladies who live in furnished souls'—29. 'i was considering how'—30. 'in Just-'—31. 'Buffalo Bill 's'—32. 'ladies and gentlemen this little girl'—33. 'into the strenuous briefness'—34. '"'kitty". sixteen, 5′ 1″, white, prostitute.'—35. 'goodby Betty, don't remember me'—36. 'the'—37. 'when you rang at Dick Mid's Place'—38. 'writhe and'—39. 'the bigness of cannon'—40. 'somebody knew Lincoln somebody Xerxes'—41. 'between nose-red gross'—42. 'the rose'—43. 'it may not always be so; and i say'—44. 'yours is the music for no instrument'—45. 'a thing most new complete fragile intense,'—46. 'my love is building a building'—47. 'notice the convulsed orange inch of moon';&°: 48. 'her'—49. 'raise the shade'—50. 'her careful distinct sex whose sharp lips comb'—51. 'between the breasts'—52. 'ta'—53. 'god pity me whom(god distinctly has)'—54. 'irreproachable ladies firmly lewd'—55. 'twentyseven bums give a prostitute the once'—56. 'Babylon slim'—57. 'she sits dropping on a caret of clenched arms'—58. 'here is little Effie's head'—59. 'of this wilting wall the colour drub'—60. 'the bed is not very big'—61. 'in making Marjorie god hurried'—62. 'fabulous against ,a,fathoming jelly'—63. 'the dirty colours of her kiss have just'—64. 'the dress was a suspicious madder, importing the cruelty of roses.'—65. 'Dick Mid's large bluish face without eyebrows'—66. 'my girl's tall with hard long eyes'—67. 'Paris; this April sunset completely utters'—68. 'impossibly'—69. 'little ladies more'—70. 'nearer:breath of my breath: take not thy tingling'—71. 'the poem her belly marched through me as'—72. 'when the spent day begins to frail'—73. 'who knows if the moon's'—74. 'inthe,exquisite;'—75. 'Spring is like a perhaps hand'—76. 'riverly is a flower'—77. 'the wind is a Lady with'—78. '(one!)'—79. 'gee i like to think of dead it means nearer because deeper'—80. 'suppose'—81. 'i will be'—82. 'of this sunset(which is so'—83. 'Take for example this:'—84. 'before the fragile gradual throne of night'—85. 'the ivory performing rose'—86. 'utterly and amusingly i am pash'—87. 'when my love comes to see me it's'—88. 'the mind is its own beautiful prisoner.'—89. 'let's

live suddenly without thinking'—90. 'i have loved, let us see if
that's all.'—91. 'my sonnet is A light goes on in'—92. 'and this
day it was Spring . . . . us'—93. 'i have found what you are like'—
94. 'if i should sleep with a lady called death'—95. 'it is funny,
you will be dead some day.'—96. 'i like my body when it is with
your'; XLI POEMS: 97. 'conversation with my friend is particularly'
—98. 'the skinny voice'—99. 'the/ sky/ was'—100. 'when i am
in Boston, i do not speak.'—101. 'Humanity i love you'—102.
'between green/ mountains'—103. 'Picasso'—104. 'little tree'—
105. 'cruelly, love'—106. 'why did you go'—107. 'into the smiting'
—108. 'when life is quite through with'—109. 'Lady of Silence'—
110. 'when unto nights of autumn do complain'—111. 'perhaps it
is to feel strike'—112. 'when learned darkness from our searched
world'—113. 'Where's Madge then,'—114. 'when my sensational
moments are no more'—115. 'this is the garden: colours come and
go,'—116. 'when the proficient poison of sure sleep'—117. 'I have
seen her a stealthily frail'—118. 'come nothing to my comparable
soul'—119. 'O Thou to whom the musical white spring'—120. 'and
what were roses. Perfume? for i do'—121. 'who's most afraid of
death? thou/ art of him'; Is 5: 122. FIVE AMERICANS: I. LIZ ('with
breathing as (faithfully) her lownecked')—II. MAME ('she puts down
the handmirror. "Look at" arranging')—III. GERT ('joggle i think
will do it although the glad')—IV. MARJ ('"life?/ Listen" the
feline she with radishred')—V. FRAN ('should i entirely ask of god
why')—123. POEM, OR BEAUTY HURTS MR. VINAL ('take it from me
kiddo')—124. 'nobody loses all the time'—125. '(and i imagine'—
126. 'curtains part)'—127. 'Jimmie's got a goil/ goil/ goil,/ Jimmie'—128. 'listen my children and you'—129. ITEM ('this man is
o so')—130. 'yonder deadfromtheneckup graduate of a'—131. ?
('why are these pipples taking their hets off?')—132. 'this young
question mark man'—133. 'mr youse needn't be so spry'—134. 'she
being Brand'—135. 'IKEY(GOLDBERG)'S WORTH I'M'—
136. ODE ('o// the sweet & aged people')—137. 'on the Madam's
best april the'—138. MEMORABILIA ('stop look &')—139. '(as that
named Fred'—140. 'my uncle'—141. 'poets yeggs and thirsties'—
142. 'a man who had fallen among thieves'—143. 'opening of the
chambers close'—144. 'the season 'tis, my lovely lambs,'—145. 'life
hurl my'—146. '16 heures'—147. '"next to of course god america
i'—148. 'my sweet old etcetera'—149. 'come, gaze with me upon
this dome'—150. 'it's jolly'—151. 'lis'—152. 'look at this)'—
153. 'than(by yon sunset's wintry glow'—154. 'but if i should say'
—155. 'Will i ever forget that precarious moment?'—156. 'candles

flower(whom'—227. 'my darling since'—228. 'because i love you)
last night'—229. 'if you and i awakening'—230. 'lady will you
come with me into'—231. 'when rain whom fear'—232. 'item:is/
Clumsily with of'—233. 'i'd think "wonder'—234. 'breathe with
me this fear'—235. 'granted the all/ saving our young kiss only'—
236. 'speaking of love(of'—237. 'be unto love as rain is unto colour;
create'—238. 'so standing,our eyes filled with wind,and the'—
239. 'nothing is more exactly terrible than'—240. 'structure,miracu-
lous challenge,devout am'—241. 'put off your faces,Death:for day
is over'—242. 'here is the ocean,this is moonlight:say'—243. 'but
if a living dance upon dead minds'; No Thanks: 244. 'o// sure)but'
—245. 'when muckers pimps and tratesmen'—246. '"let's start a
magazine'—247. 'he does not have to feel because he thinks'—
248. 'this little'—249. 'o pr'—250. 'may i feel said he'—251. 'kumrads die because they're told)'—252. 'worshipping Same'—
253. 'that which we who're alive in spite of mirrors'—254. 'little
man'—255. 'sonnet entitled how to run the world)'—256. 'brIght'
—257. 'most(people'—258. 'Jehovah buried,Satan dead,'—
259. 'into a truly'—260. 'exit a kind of unkindness exit'—261. 'little
joe gould has lost his teeth and doesn't know where'—262. 'sh
estiffl'—263. 'floatfloaflofif'—264. 'out of a supermetamathical
subpreincestures'—265. 'they sO alive/(who is/?niggers)'—
266. 'death(having lost)put on his universe'—267. 'does yesterday's
perfection seem not quite'—268. 'how dark and single,where he
ends,the earth'—269. 'here's to opening and upward,to leaf and to
sap'—270. '(b/eLl/s?/bE'—271. 'love is a place'—272. 'at dusk/
just when'—273. 'birds(/here,inven'—274. 'mouse)Won'—
275. 'go(perpe)go'—276. 'r-p-o-p-h-e-s-s-a-g-r'—277. 'mOOn Over
tOwns mOOn'—278. 'love's function is to fabricate unknownness'
—279. 'Do.'—280. 'Spring(side'—281. 'what a proud dreamhorse
pulling(smoothloomingly) through'—282. 'this mind made war'—
283. 'sometimes/ in)Spring a someone will lie(glued'—284. 'when/
from a sidewalk/ out of(blown never quite to'—285. 'silent unday
by silently not night'—286. 'come(all you mischief-'—287. 'be of
love(a little)'—288. 'much i cannot)'—289. 'move'—290. 'if night's
mostness(and whom did merely day'—291. 'reason let others give
and realness bring—'—292. 'morsel miraculous and meaningless'—
293. 'conceive a man,should he have anything'; New Poems: 294.
'un'—295. 'kind)'—296. 'a football with white eyebrows the'
—297. '(of Ever-Ever Land i speak'—298. 'lucky means finding'—
299. 'Q:dwo'—300. '&-moon-He-be-hind-a-mills'—301. 'this little
bride & groom are'—302. 'so little he is'—303. 'nor woman/(just

E. E. Cummings

as it be'—304. 'my specialty is living said'—305. 'The Mind's('—306. 'if i'—307. 'hanged'—308. 'economic secu'—309. 'beware beware beware'—310. 'only as what(out of a flophouse)floats'—311. 'must being shall'—312. 'may my heart always be open to little'—313. 'the people who'—314. 'porky & porkie'—315. 'you shall above all things be glad and young.'.

A18   50 POEMS   [1940]

a. First edition, limited issue:

50 | POEMS | [*double rule*] | [*facsimile signature*] E. E. C's | DUELL, SLOAN AND PEARCE | NEW YORK

[109]pp., 1 blank leaf. $5\frac{1}{2} \times 8\frac{3}{4}$ inches. $5.00. Beige cloth with dark brown leather label stamped in gold on front cover and stamped in gold down spine; flat spine; end papers. Beige cloth covered slip case with brown paper label printed in gold on side.

Colophon (verso of title page): THIS EDITION IS LIMITED TO 150 COPIES, OF WHICH THIS IS COPY NUMBER ... [signed, recto of front end paper] E. E. C's

Published on December 18, 1940.

Contents: 1. '!blac'—2. 'fl'—3. 'If you can't eat you got to'—4. 'nobody loved this'—5. 'am was. are leaves few this. is these a or'—6. 'flotsam and jetsam'—7. 'moan'—8. 'the Noster was a ship of swank'—9. 'warped this perhapsy'—10. 'spoke joe to jack'—11. 'red-rag and pink-flag'—12. '(will you teach a'—13. 'proud of his scientific attitude'—14. 'the way to hump a cow is not'—15. 'mrs'—16. ')when what hugs stopping earth than silent is'—17. 'youful'—18. 'ecco a letter starting "dearest we"'—19. 'there is a here and'—20. 'harder perhaps than a newengland bed'—21. 'six'—22. 'nouns to nouns'—23. 'a pretty a day'—24. 'these people socalled were not given hearts'—25. 'as freedom is a break-fastfood'—26. 'wherelings whenlings'—27. 'buy me an ounce and i'll sell you a pound.'—28. 'there are possibly $2\frac{1}{2}$ or impossibly 3'—29. 'anyone lived in a pretty how town'—30. 'the silently little blue elephant shyly(he was terri'—31. 'not time's how(anchored in what mountaining roots'—32. 'newlys of silence'—33. 'one slip-slouch twi'—34. 'my father moved through dooms of love'—35. 'you which could grin three smiles into a dead'—36. 'i say no world'—37. 'these children singing in stone a'—38. 'love is the every only god'—40. 'a peopleshaped toomany-ness far too'—

28

41. 'up into the silence the green'—42. 'love is more thicker than forget'—43. 'hate blows a bubble of despair into'—44. 'air,'—45. 'enters give'—46. 'grEEn's d'—47. '(sitting in a tree-)'—48. 'mortals)'—49. 'i am so glad and very'—50. 'what freedom's not some under's mere above'.

b. Ordinary issue ([1941]):

[111]pp. $5\frac{3}{8} \times 8\frac{7}{16}$ inches. $1.50. Light tan cloth stamped in brown on front cover and down spine; end papers. Light tan dust wrapper printed in brown.

1000 copies published on January 10, 1941. Second and third printings, with smaller page dimensions and bound in reddish tan cloth, are noted on the front flap of the dust wrapper.

Among the periodicals listed in the acknowledgments on page [7] is one entitled *Poetry Weekly.* I believe this is a misprint for *Poetry World,* a magazine not credited with a prior publication of a poem collected in this volume for the first time.

c. Second edition ([1960]):

50 | POEMS | [*facsimile signature*] E. E. C's | [*rule*] | *The Universal Library* | GROSSET & DUNLAP | NEW YORK

[111], [13] pp., 1 blank leaf. $5\frac{3}{8} \times 8$ inches. 95 cents. White wrapper printed in orange, magenta, blue and black; sewn.

10,000 copies published on January 18, 1960, as UL-66 in The Universal Library.

Contents same as the first edition.

A19   ONE TIMES ONE   [1944]

a. First edition:

E E CUMMINGS | [*rule*] | I × I | NEW YORK : HENRY HOLT AND COMPANY

[77], [1]pp. $5\frac{3}{8} \times 8\frac{3}{8}$ inches. $2.00. Gray cloth stamped in royal blue down and across spine; end papers. White dust wrapper printed in black ("Self-portrait" by Cummings on back).

2500 copies published on March 13, 1944. Second and Third printing noted on verso of title page.

Contents: 1: I. 'nonsun blob a'—II. 'neither could say'—III. 'it's over a(see just'—IV. 'of all the blessings which to man'—V. 'squints a blond'—VI. 'my(his from daughter's mother's zero

mind'—VII. 'ygUDuh'—VIII. 'applaws)'—IX. 'a salesman is an
it that stinks Excuse'—X. 'a politician is an arse upon'—XI. 'mr
u will not be missed'—XII. 'it was a goodly co'—XIII. 'plato told'
—XIV. 'pity this buy monster,manunkind,'—XV. '("fire stop
thief help murder save the world"'—XVI. 'one's not half two.
It's two are halves of one:'; x: XVII. 'one(Floatingly)arrive'—
XVIII. 'as any(men's hells having wrestled with)'—XIX. 'when
you are silent,shining host by guest'—XX. 'what if a much of a
which of a wind'—XXI. 'dead every enormous piece'—XXII. 'no
man,if men are gods;but if gods must'—XXIII. 'love is a spring at
which'—XXIV. '(once like a spark)'—XXV. 'what over and which
under'—XXVI. 'when god decided to invent'—XXVII. 'old mr ly'
—XXVIII. 'rain or hail'—XXIX. 'let it go—the'—XXX. 'Hello
is what a mirror says'—XXXI. 'a-'—XXXII. 'i've come to ask
you if there isn't a'—XXXIII. 'open green those'—XXXIV. 'nothing false and possible is love'—XXXV. 'except in your'—
XXXVI. 'true lovers in each happening of their hearts'—
XXXVII. 'we love each other very dearly/,more'—XXXVIII. 'yes
is a pleasant country:'—XXXIX. 'all ignorance toboggans into
know'—XL. 'darling!because my blood can sing'; 1: XLI. 'how//
tinily'—XLII. 'might these be thrushes climbing through almost(do
they'—XLIII. 'if(among'—XLIV. 'these(whom;pretends'—XLV.
'i think you like"'—XLVI. 'open your heart:'—XLVII. 'until
and i heard'—XLVIII. 'so isn't small one littlest why,'—XLIX.
'trees/ were in(give'—L. 'which is the very'—LI. '"sweet spring
in your'—LII. 'life is more true than reason will deceive'—LIII. 'o
by the by'—LIV. 'if everything happens that can't be done'.

b. First English edition ([*1947*]):

E E CUMMINGS | [*rule*] | 1 × 1 | WITH AN INTRODUCTION
BY LLOYD FRANKENBERG | LONDON : HORIZON

[83], [1]pp. front. ("E. E. CUMMINGS. *Self-portrait*"). $5\frac{3}{8} \times 8\frac{1}{2}$
inches. 8s. 6d. Yellow cloth stamped in blue on spine; end papers.
Cream dust wrapper printed in magenta.

Published on October 14, 1947. *On verso of title page:* First published
(*Holt*, New York) 1944 New edition published by *Horizon* 1947

Contents are the same as the first American edition except for the
use of single quotes for double quotes in the text of the poems and
the addition of Mr. Frankenberg's essay, "Introduction: nothing
as something as one", pp. [9]–[20]. "nothing as something as one"
first appeared in *The Harvard Wake*, no. 5 (Spring 1946), 46–54.

A : Books

c. Second American edition ([*1954*]):

E E CUMMINGS | [*rule*] | 1 × 1 | NEW YORK : HARCOURT, BRACE AND COMPANY

[77], [1]pp. 5¼ × 8 inches. $2.75. Light olive cloth stamped in silver down spine; end papers. White dust wrapper printed in dark green.

1500 copies published on June 3, 1954.

Contents same as first American edition.

A20   ANTHROPOS   [1944]

First edition:

AN | THROPOS | *The Future of Art* [Mt. Vernon, New York: The Golden Eagle Press]

1 blank leaf, [26]pp., 1 leaf, 1 blank leaf; the whole interleaved with 14 leaves of black paper. 7½ × 10¾ inches. $7.50. Black cloth with white paper strip on front cover printed in black and white paper label on spine printed down in black; flat spine; end papers. White paper covered slip case.

Colophon (recto of last leaf): This is an editio princeps *of the author's contribution to a symposium, and it consists of 222 copies, printed on Arnold Unbleached all rag mould made paper. S. A. Jacobs at The Golden Eagle Press, Fleetwood, Mount Vernon, New York.*

Published in 1944.

A21   SANTA CLAUS   [1946]

a. First edition, ordinary issue:

SANTA | CLAUS | *A Morality by* | E. E. CUMMINGS | NEW YORK : HENRY HOLT AND COMPANY

1 blank leaf, 5 leaves, 18, [1]pp. 7⅜ × 10⅝ inches. $1.50. Scarlet cloth over boards, black cloth back, stamped in gold on black cloth on cover and down spine; flat spine; end papers. White dust wrapper printed in black and red ("*self portrait*" by Cummings on back).

1500 copies published on December 1, 1946. Second printing noted on verso of title page.

b. Limited issue:

[*In red:*] SANTA | CLAUS | [*in black:*] *A Morality by* | E. E. CUMMINGS | NEW YORK : HENRY HOLT AND COMPANY

E. E. Cummings

1 blank leaf, 5 leaves, 18 pp., 1 blank leaf, incl. front. ([Self portrait with mask], a line drawing by Cummings). $5.00. Glassine dust wrapper.

Colophon (recto of second leaf): Of this book, designed by Maurice Serle Kaplan and set in Weiss types by the Composing Room, Inc., 250 copies have been specially printed by Aldus Printers and signed by the author, of which this is No. . . . [*signed on recto of first end paper*] E. E. C's

Published on December 1, 1946.

In this issue the names of the speakers are printed in red, the text of what is spoken in black. In the ordinary issue both are printed in black.

A22   PUELLA MEA   [1949]

First edition:

[*On left hand page: a drawing by Paul Klee*] | PUELLA MEA | [*on right hand page:*] BY E. E. CUMMINGS | [*a painting by Paul Klee*] | COPYRIGHT MCMXXIII   BY   E   E   CUMMINGS PRINTED IN THE UNITED STATES OF AMERICA [Mt. Vernon, New York: The Golden Eagle Press]

2 blank leaves, [23], [1]pp., 2 blank leaves. $4\frac{3}{4} \times 8$ inches. Blue gray paper over boards stamped in gold on front cover and up spine; flat spine; end papers. Blue gray dust wrapper printed in gold and gold paper covered slip case.

Colophon (p. [24]): This edition of E. E. Cummings' Puella Mea with reproductions of drawings and paintings by Klee is made possible through the kind permission of Curt Valentin of Buchholz Gallery. The Modigliani drawing is used by the courtesy of his publishers, in Milan, Italy. For the drawing by Picasso thanks are due to Mary Callery, who consented to its use. Kurt Roesch contributed his drawing which is the only illustration expressly made for this book when it was decided to have work by other modern masters in addition to the one drawing by the author himself, which appears on the first text page of his poem. s. a. jacobs, the golden eagle press

This is the first separate printing of puella mea ('Harun Omar and Master Hafiz'). It was first published in book form in *Tulips and Chimneys*.

32

A : Books

XAIPE

First edition:

[*In blue:*] XAIPE | [*in black:*] seventy-one poems | by e e cummings | new york [*publisher's device in blue*] | oxford university press 1950

2 blank leaves, ix, 1 leaf, [72]pp., 2 blank leaves. $5\frac{3}{8} \times 8$ inches. $2.50. Powder blue paper over boards stamped in blind on front cover and in silver down and across spine. Powder blue dust wrapper printed in black and gray.

2500 copies published on March 30, 1950. Second printing noted on verso of title page.

Contents: 1. 'this(let's remember)day died again and'—2. 'hush)' —3. 'purer than purest pure'—4. 'this out of within itself moo'— 5. 'swim so now million many worlds in each'—6. 'dying is fine) but Death'—7. 'we miss you,jack—tactfully you(with one cocked' —8. 'o// the round'—9. 'possibly thrice we glimpsed—/more likely twice'—10. 'or who and who)'—11. 'so many selves(so many fiends and gods'—12. 'tw'—13. 'chas sing does(who'— 14. 'out of more find than seeks'—15. 'hair your a brook'—16. 'if the'—17. '(swooming)a pillar of youngly'—18. 'a(ncient)a'— 19. 'out of the mountain of his soul comes'—20. 'goo-dmore-ning (en'—21. 'jake hates/all the girls(the'—22. 'when serpents bargain for the right to squirm'—23. 'three wealthy sisters swore they'd never part:'—24. 'one day a nigger'—25. 'pieces(in darker'— 26. 'who sharpens every dull'—27. '"summer is over'—28. 'noone" autumnal this great lady's gaze'—29. 'nine birds(rising'—30. 'snow means that"'—31. 'infinite jukethrob smoke & swallow to dis'— 32. 'blossoming are people'—33. 'if a cheerfulest Elephantangel-child should sit'—34. 'a thrown a'—35. 'light's lives lurch/ a once world quickly from rises'—36. 'quick i the death of thing'—37. 'F is for foetus(a'—38. 'why must itself up every of a park'—39. 'open his head,baby'—40. 'i'm'—41. 'whose are these(wraith a cling-ing with a wraith)'—42. 'neither awake'—43. 'o to be in finland'— 44. 'where's Jack Was'—45. 'when your honest redskin toma'— 46. 'a kike is the most dangerous'—47. 'meet mr universe(who clean'—48. '&(all during the'—49. 'this is a rubbish of human rind'—50. 'no time ago'—51. 'who were so dark of heart they might not speak,'—52. 'to start,to hesitate;to stop'—53. 'mighty guest of merely me'—54. 'maybe god'—55. '(fea'—56. 'a like a'— 57. '(im)c-a-t(mo)'— 58. 'after screamgroa'—59. 'the little horse

33

is newlY'—60. '(nothing whichful about'—61. 'if(touched by love's own secret)we,like homing'—62. 'in'—63. 'honour corruption villainy holiness'—64. 'the of an it ignoblest he'—65. 'i thank You God for most this amazing'—66. 'the great advantage of being alive'—67. 'when faces called flowers float out of the ground'—68. 'love our so right'—69. 'now all the fingers of this tree(darling) have'—70. 'blue the triangular why'—71. 'luminous tendril of celestial wish'.

A24   i: SIX NONLECTURES   1953

a. First edition, ordinary issue:

[*On left hand page:*] *e e cummings* i [*on right hand page:*] SIX NON-LECTURES | harvard university press | cambridge 1953

4 leaves, 118pp., 1 blank leaf. 5¾ × 9¼ inches. $3.00. Black cloth stamped in white down spine; end papers. White dust wrapper printed in black (photograph of Cummings by Marion Morehouse on back).

4650 copies published on November 12, 1953. Second printing noted on verso of title page.

Contents: NONLECTURE ONE: i & my parents—NONLECTURE TWO: i & their son—NONLECTURE THREE: i & selfdiscovery—NONLECTURE FOUR: i & you & is—NONLECTURE FIVE: i & now & him—NONLECTURE SIX: i & am & santa claus.

In addition to liberal quotation from Cummings' books, the *Nonlectures* contain the following published, but uncollected, items: (pp. 8–9) [Part of a Letter to Paul Rosenfeld]—(p. 64) An Imaginary Dialogue between an Author and a Public—(p. 67) Anno Domini 1940—(p. 68) Foreword [American British Art Center catalogue, 1944]—(p. 69) Re Ezra Pound—(pp. 69–70) Is Something Wrong [in part].

b. Limited issue:

5 leaves, 118pp., 1 blank leaf. $6.50. Black cloth over boards, white cloth back, stamped in black on spine; flat spine; end papers. Dust wrapper as on ordinary issue.

Colophon (*verso of first leaf*): Number . . . of an edition limited to 350 copies [*signed*] E. E. C's

Published on November 12, 1953.

A : Books

A25   POEMS 1923-1954   [1954]

First edition:

E. E. CUMMINGS | Poems | 1923-1954 | HARCOURT, BRACE AND COMPANY · NEW YORK

xxiv, 468pp. 2 blank leaves. 6 × 9¼ inches. $6.75. Coral cloth stamped in silver and maroon on front cover and spine; end papers; top edges stained maroon. White dust wrapper printed in red, gold and black (photograph of Cummings by Marion Morehouse on front).

10,000 copies published on October 28, 1954. *On verso of title page:* . . . first edition . . . Later printings noted on verso of title page by means of code letters "B", "C", etc. Copies printed for distribution to members of The Readers' Subscription lack printing notice.

This volume brings together all of the poems first published in *Tulips and Chimneys, XLI Poems, &°, Is 5, ViVa, No Thanks, Collected Poems, 50 Poems, 1 × 1* and *Xaipe.*

NOTE: The second and third printings of *Poems 1923-1954* incorporate many textual changes and corrections made by the author. These are listed below. Unstarred items denote changes and corrections made in the second printing; starred (*) items in the third. For present purposes, all lines are counted, even those that do not flush left.

EPITHALAMION, p. 6, line 15: for "e'er" read "ere".
SONGS I, p. 9, line 15: for "e'er" read "ere".
PUELLA MEA, p. 14, line 30: for "Salome" read "Salomé".
PUELLA MEA, p. 20, line 2: for "alway" read "always".
ORIENTALE VI, p. 28, line 13: for "ancus" read "ankus".
LA GUERRE I, p. 39, line 9: for "silence" read "silence.".
IMPRESSIONS III, p. 42, line 12: move line one space to right.
PORTRAITS IX, p. 51, lines 19-20: delete line space between lines.
PORTRAITS IX, p. 51, line 32: for "screetch" read "screech".
PORTRAITS IX, p. 51, lines 33-34: insert line space between lines.
*POST IMPRESSIONS VI, p. 57, line 7: for "fattish" read "fatish".
POST IMPRESSIONS VI, p. 57, line 26: for "his my" read "myhis".
SONNETS—REALITIES III, p. 59, line 14: for "abslatively" read "absitively".
SONNETS—UNREALITIES V, p. 63, line 12: for "air!)Let" read "air!) Let".
*SONNETS—ACTUALITIES V, p. 67, line 9: for "cherie" read "chérie".
POST IMPRESSIONS IV, p. 75, line 10: move line one space to left.

35

E. E. Cummings

POST IMPRESSIONS V, p. 75, line 1: for "Paris:" read "Paris;".

POST IMPRESSIONS XIV, p. 84, lines 14–15: insert line space between lines.

PORTRAITS V, p. 88, line 20: move line two spaces to right and for "oo-oo. dearie" read "oo-oo.   dearie".

PORTRAITS IX, p. 95, line 3: for "terriculous" read "terricolous".

*PORTRAITS XII, p. 98, line 6: for "pourquoi?" read "pourquoi?)".

PORTRAITS XII, p. 98, line 19: for "de" read "des".

PORTRAITS XII, p. 98, line 20: move line one space to left.

*PORTRAITS XII, p. 98, line 33: move line one space to left.

&: SEVEN POEMS I, p. 99, line 9: for ". . . . kIss" read ". . . .kIss".

&: SEVEN POEMS I, p. 99, line 28: move line one space to left.

SONNETS—REALITIES VIII, p. 108, line 28: move line one space to right.

SONNETS—REALITIES VIII, p. 109, line 5: move line one space to right.

SONNETS—REALITIES XXI, p. 115, line 15: for "annihilation." read "annihilation".

SONNETS—ACTUALITIES IV, p. 118, line 7: move line one space to left.

SONNETS—ACTUALITIES XIII, p. 123, line 14: for "bulleying" read "bullying".

SONNETS I, p. 152, line 1: for "when" read "if".

SONNETS I, p. 152, line 2: for "wrestest" read "should wrest".

SONNETS I, p. 152, line 3: for "if thy two" read "and if thy".

SONNETS I, p. 152, line 4: for "thought" read "wish".

SONNETS I, p. 152, line 5: for "dreamest" read "dreams".

SONNETS I, p. 152, line 6: for "—proud" read "(proud".

SONNETS I, p. 152, line 7: for "thou seemest" read "she seems".

SONNETS I, p. 152, line 8: for "(whose" read "whose".

SONNETS I, p. 153, line 7: for "shalt thou" read "could we".

SONNETS IV, p. 154, line 9: for "reap," read "reap".

SONNETS XVI, p. 160, line 2: for "screetch" read "screech".

ONE: I (FIVE AMERICANS: III GERT), p. 166, line 12: move line one space to right.

ONE: I (FIVE AMERICANS: III GERT), p. 166, line 13: move line one space to right.

ONE: II (POEM, OR BEAUTY HURTS MR. VINAL), p. 167, line 6: for "Eyes(of" read "Eyes (of".

ONE: II (POEM, OR BEAUTY HURTS MR. VINAL), p. 168, line 12: for "me?)according" read "me?) according".

ONE: II (POEM, OR BEAUTY HURTS MR. VINAL), p. 168, line 15: for "formula:example" read "formula: example".

ONE: II (POEM, OR BEAUTY HURTS MR. VINAL), p. 168, line 26: for "gelded(or" read "gelded (or".

A : Books

ONE: II (POEM, OR BEAUTY HURTS MR. VINAL), p. 168, line 27: for
"gentlemen(and" read "gentlemen (and".

ONE: II (POEM, OR BEAUTY HURTS MR. VINAL), p. 168, line 30: for
"americans(who" read "americans (who".

ONE: II (POEM, OR BEAUTY HURTS MR. VINAL), p. 168, line 35: for
"nuisance:Odor?" read "nuisance: Odor?".

ONE: III, p. 169, line 3: for "Flo"s" read "Flo's".

ONE: IV, p. 170, line 12: for "Mæterlink" read "Maeterlinck".

ONE: XVI (?), p. 176, line 4: for "Hotel" read "Hôtel".

ONE: XIX, p. 178, line 21: for "greasedlightning just" read
"greasedlightning)just".

ONE: XXXII, p. 188, line 27: for "spitoon" read "spittoon".

TWO: III, p. 193, line 13: for "voices" read "voice".

THREE: II, p. 199, line 14: move line one space to right.

THREE: III, p. 200, line 19: for "Jaqueline" read "Jacqueline".

THREE: V, p. 202, line 23: move line one space to right.

FOUR: I, p. 205, lines 8–9: insert line space between lines.

FOUR: II, p. 205, line 1: for "morticed" read "mortised".

FOUR: VIII, p. 209, line 14: move line one space to left.

FIVE: III, p. 218, line 10: for "cheri" read "chéri".

FIVE: V, p. 219, line 1: for "made, my lady, intricate" read
"made,my lady,intricate".

POEM X, p. 230, line 8: for "-with -the -chinese-" read
"-with-the-chinese-".

POEM XI, p. 231, line 22: move line one space to left.

POEM XVII, p. 236, line 7: for "babbit" read "babbitt".

POEM XXXI, p. 245, line 3: for "dormas" read "dormers".

POEM XLIII, p. 253, line 3: for "lilies-of the-valley" read
"lilies-of-the-valley".

*POEM XLIII, p. 253, line 8: for "swaying" read "(swaying".

POEM XLV, p. 255, line 14: for "cary" read "carry".

*POEM XLVI, p. 256, line 21: for "town" read "town)".

POEM XLIX, p. 258, line 6: for "Fndingest" read "Findingest".

POEM LI, p. 259, line 5: for "e'er" read "ere".

POEM 5, p. 280, line 1: for "i(meet)t(touch)" read
"i// (meet)t(touch)".

POEM 22, p. 365, line 4: for "two" read "too".

POEM XXIII, p. 402, line 10: for "those" read "these".

Mr. Cummings' publisher has informed me that an additional
change will be made in the fourth printing of *Poems 1923–1954*, as
follows:

POEM VII, p. 393, lines 2–9: move lines one space to right.

E. E. Cummings

a. First edition, ordinary issue:

E. E. CUMMINGS | A MISCELLANY | Edited, with an introduction and notes, by | GEORGE J. FIRMAGE | FOREWORD BY THE AUTHOR | 1958 | The Argophile Press: New York

  xi, 241pp., 1 leaf, incl. illus. 2 plates (incl. front.—photograph of Cummings by Marion Morehouse). 6 × 9 inches. $6.50. Dark blue cloth stamped in silver on front cover and down spine; flat spine; light gray end papers. Glassine dust wrapper.

  977 copies published on May 31, 1958. *On verso of title page: . . . First Edition . . .*

  This edition exists in two states: (1) 564 copies—400 with illustration on p. 42 ("Piano Player") printed upright and 164 with illustration tilting downward to the right; (2) 413 copies with illustration printed upright on a tipped-in leaf.

  50 advance copies for review, bound in plain grey cloth, were issued two weeks prior to the book's publication date. *On inside back cover end paper (in blue ink):* Review copy: No. . . . of 50

  Contents: Introduction (by George J. Firmage)—Foreword (by E. E. Cummings)—ETCETERA: Jottings—Videlicet—Foreword: I—Foreword: II—Foreword: III—Words Into Pictures—Fair Warning—A Poet's Advice to Students; APPRECIATIONS: The New Art—Gaston Lachaise ([A note about Gaston Lachaise])—T. S. Eliot—Jean Cocteau As a Graphic Artist—The Adult, The Artist and The Circus—"I Take Great Pleasure In Presenting"—Coney Island—Conflicting Aspects of Paris—Vive la Folie!—You Aren't Mad, Am I? ("The Jew Comedian", "Cleo", "Dance du Ventre", line drawings by Cummings)—The Theatre: I—The Theatre: II—The Secret of the Zoo Exposed—Miracles and Dreams—The Agony of the Artist (With a Capital A)—Burlesque, I Love It!—Why I Like America ("La 'Beauté' Francaise", a line drawing by Cummings)—A Fairy Tale—A Foreword to Krazy; VANITY FAIR: The Soul Story of Gladys Vanderdecker—Vanity Fair's Prize Movie-Scenario—What Our Loving Subscribers Say—An Ex-Multimillionaire's Rules For Success in Life—A Modern Gulliver Explores the Movies—When Calvin Coolidge Laughed—William Adams-Wiggley: Genius and Christian—Seven Samples of Dramatic Criticism—Unexpected Light on the Dawes Plan—How To Succeed as an Author—The Very Latest School in Art—Helen Whiffletree, American Poetess—"I Confess!"

—How I Do Not Love Italy—The Tabloid Newspaper—Frenzied Finance—Ivan Narb: Abstract Sculptor of the Cosmic—The New Mother Goose—Mr. X—In Memoriam—Exit the Boob—What About It?—And It Came to Pass—Weligion Is Hashish—BALLAD OF AN INTELLECTUAL ('Listen, you morons great and small'); FROM AN UNFINISHED PLAY: Speech: I—Speech: II—Speech: III.

b. Limited issue:

Extra leaf tipped-in between pp. [ii] and [iii]. $10.00. Light gray cloth stamped in blue on front cover and down spine; flat spine; end papers. Glassine dust wrapper.

Colophon (recto of tipped-in leaf): This edition of E. E. Cummings: A Miscellany is limited to 75 copies numbered and signed by the author of which this is copy number . . . [signed] E. E. C's May 31, 1958

Published on May 31, 1958.

The illustration on p. 42 is printed tilting downward to the right in ten copies of this issue; it is printed upright in all other copies.

A27   95 POEMS   [1958]

a. First edition, limited issue:

95 | poems by e. e. cummings | harcourt, brace & company | new york | [*publisher's device*]

[114]pp. 5¾ × 9 inches. $12.00. Blue cloth stamped in blind on front cover, spine and back cover, and in gold on front cover and spine; flat spine; yellow end papers; top edges stained yellow. Glassine dust wrapper and black paper covered slip case with white paper label printed in gold on side and back.

Colophon (p. [3]): The first edition of 95 poems is limited to three hundred numbered copies on rag paper, signed by e. e. cummings, of which two hundred and eighty are for sale. This is number . . . [signed] E. E. C's

Published on October 8, 1958.

Errors in the acknowledgments on the verso of the title page were corrected in the second printing of the ordinary issue.

Contents: 1. 'l(a'—2. 'to stand(alone)in some'—3. 'now air is air and thing is thing:no bliss'—4. 'this man's heart'—5. 'crazy jay blue)'—6. 'spirit colossal'—7. 'because you take life in your stride (instead'—8. 'dominic has'—9. 'both eaching come ghostlike'—10. 'maggie and milly and molly and may'—11. 'in time's a noble

E. E. Cummings

mercy of proportion'—12. 'lily has a rose'—13. 'So shy shy shy(and
with a'—14. 'but also dying'—15. 'on littlest this'—16. 'in time
of daffodils(who know'—17. 'for prodigal read generous'—18. 'once
White&Gold'—19. 'un(bee)mo'—20. 'off a pane)the'—21. 'joys
faces friends'—22. 'why from this her and him'—23. 'albutnotquitemost'—24. 'dim'—25. 'that melancholy'—26. 'round a so
moon could dream(i sus'—27. 'jack's white horse(up'—28. 'as joe
gould says in'—29. 'ev erythingex Cept:'—30. 'what Got him was
Noth'—31. 'a he as o'—32. 'who(at'—33. 'a gr'—34. ADHUC SUB
JUDICE LIS ('when mack smacked phyllis on the snout')—35. '"so
you're hunting for ann well i'm looking for will"'—36. 'yes but
even'—37. 'handsome and clever and he went cruising'—38. 's.
ti:rst;hiso,nce;ma:n'—39. THANKSGIVING (1956) ('a monstering horror swallows')—40. 'silence'—41. 'Beautiful'—42. 'from spiralling
ecstatically this'—43. 'who(is?are)who'—44. '—laughing to find'
—45. 'i love you much(most beautiful darling)'—46. 'never could
anyone'—47. 'out of night's almosT Floats a colour(in'—48. 'someone i am wandering a town(if its'—49. 'noone and a star stand,am
to am'—50. '!'—51. 'f'—52. 'why'—53. 'n'—54. 'ardensteil-
henarub-izabeth)'—55. 'you no'—56. 'home means that'—57. 'old
age sticks'—58. 'a total stranger one black day'—59. 'when any
mortal(even the most odd)'—60. 'dive for dreams'—61. 'Young
m'—62. 'your birthday comes to tell me this'—63. 'precisely as
unbig as why as i'm'—64. 'out of the lie of no'—65. 'first robin
the;'—66. '"but why should"'—67. 'this little huge'—68. 'the
(oo)is'—69. 'over us if(as what was duck becomes'—70. 'whatever's merely wilful,'—71. 'stand with your lover on the ending
earth—'—72. 'i shall imagine life'—73. 'let's,from some loud unworld's most rightful wrong'—74. 'sentinel robins two'—75. '(hills
chime with thrush)'—76. 'these from my mother's greatgrandmother's rosebush white'—77. 'i am a little church(no great
cathedral)'—78. 'all nearness pauses,while a star can grow'—
79. 'whippoorwill this'—80. 'if the Lovestar grows most big'
—81. 'here's s'—82. 'now comes the good rain farmers pray for
(and'—83. 'perished have safe small'—84. 'how generous is that
himself the sun'—85. 'here pasture ends—'—86. 'this'—87. 'now
(more near ourselves than we)'—88. 'joyful your complete fearless
and pure love'—89. 'now what were motionless move(exists no'—
90. 'rosetree, rosetree'—91. 'unlove's the heavenless hell and homeless home'—92. 'i carry your heart with me(i carry it in'—
93. 'spring!may—'—94. 'being to timelessness as it's to time,'—95.
'if up's the word;and a world grows greener'.

A : Books

b. Ordinary issue:

[112]pp. $4.00. Light brown paper printed in black over boards, polished black cloth back, stamped in dusty rose down spine; flat spine; end papers. White dust wrapper printed in black, blue and dusty rose.

5000 copies published on October 8, 1958. *On verso of title page:*
. . . FIRST EDITION AFTER PRINTING 300 COPIES OF LIMITED EDITION . . .
Later printings noted on verso of title page by means of code letters
"B", "C", etc.

The publisher has informed me that a correction will be made in the third printing of *95 Poems*, as follows: POEM 33, line 15: for "(hfraiduh)" read "(hfraiduh".

A28   100 SELECTED POEMS   [1959]

First edition:

100 Selected Poems | by e. e. cummings | Grove Press, Inc. New York

1 blank leaf, 6 leaves, 121 pp. $5\frac{1}{4} \times 7\frac{7}{8}$ inches. $1.45. White wrapper printed in black, purple and ochre; sewn.

5000 copies published on November 4, 1959, as Evergreen Book E-190, *On verso of title page:* . . . FIRST EVERGREEN EDITION 1959 . . .
Second printing noted on verso of title page.

Contents: 1. 'Thy fingers make early flowers of'—2. 'All in green went my love riding'—3. 'when god lets my body be'—4. 'in Just-'—5. 'O sweet spontaneous'—6. 'Buffalo Bill 's'—7. 'the Cambridge ladies who live in furnished souls'—8. 'it may not always be so; and i say'—9. 'suppose'—10. 'raise the shade'—11. 'here is little Effie's head'—12. 'Spring is like a perhaps hand'—13. 'who knows if the moon's'—14. 'i like my body when it is with your'—15. 'little tree'—16. 'Humanity i love you'—17. POEM, OR BEAUTY HURTS MR. VINAL ('take it from me kiddo')—18. 'nobody loses all the time'—19. 'mr youse needn't be so spry'—20. 'she being Brand'—21. MEMORABILIA ('stop look & ')—22. 'a man who had fallen among thieves'—23. 'voices to voices, lip to lip'—24. '"next to of course god america i'—25. 'my sweet old etcetera'—26. 'here's a little mouse)and'—27. 'in spite of everything'—28. 'since feeling is first'—29. 'if i have made,my lady,intricate'—30. 'i sing of Olaf glad and big'—31. 'if there are any heavens my mother will(all by herself)have'—32. 'a light Out)/ & first of all foam'—33. 'a clown's smirk in the skull of a baboon'—34. 'if i love You'—35. 'somewhere i have never travelled,gladly beyond'—36. 'but if a living

41

E. E. Cummings

dance upon dead minds'—37. 'sonnet entitled how to run the world)'—38. 'may i feel said he'—39. 'little joe gould has lost his teeth and doesn't know where'—40. 'kumrads die because they're told)'—41. 'conceive a man,should he have anything'—42. 'here's to opening and upward,to leaf and to sap'—43. 'what a proud dreamhorse pulling(smoothloomingly)through'—44. 'Jehovah buried,Satan dead,'—45. 'this mind made war'—46. 'love's function is to fabricate unknownness'—47. 'death(having lost)put on his universe'—48. 'kind)'—49. '(of Ever-Ever Land i speak'—50. 'this little bride & groom are'—51. 'my specialty is living said'—52. 'if i'—53. 'may my heart always be open to little'—54. 'you shall above all things be glad and young.'—55. 'flotsam and jetsam'—56. 'spoke joe to jack'—57. 'red-rag and pink-flag'—58. 'proud of his scientific attitude'—59. 'a pretty a day'—60. 'as freedom is a breakfastfood'—61. 'anyone lived in a pretty how town'—62. 'my father moved through dooms of love'—63. 'i say no world'—64. 'these children singing in stone a'—65. 'love is the every only god'—66. 'love is more thicker than forget'—67. 'hate blows a bubble of despair into'—68. 'what freedom's not some under's mere above'—69. 'of all the blessings which to man'—70. 'a salesman is an it that stinks Excuse'—71. 'a politician is an arse upon'—72. 'plato told'—73. 'pity this busy monster,manunkind,'—74. 'one's not half two. It's two are halves of one:'—75. 'what if a much of a which of a wind'—76. 'no man,if men are gods;but if gods must'—77. 'when god decided to invent'—78. 'rain or hail'—79. 'let it go—the'—80. 'nothing false and possible is love'—81. 'except in your'—82. 'true lovers in each happening of their hearts'—83. 'yes is a pleasant country:'—84. 'all ignorance toboggans into know'—85. 'darling!because my blood can sing'—86. '"sweet spring is your'—87. 'o by the by'—88. 'if everything happens that can't be done'—89. 'when serpents bargain for the right to squirm'—90. 'if a cheerfulest Elephantangelchild should sit'—91. 'o to be in finland'—92. 'no time ago'—93. 'to start,to hesitate;to stop'—94. 'if(touched by love's own secret)we,like homing'—95. 'i thank You God for most this amazing'—96. 'the great advantage of being alive'—97. 'when faces called flowers float out of the ground'—98. 'love our so right'—99. 'now all the fingers of this tree(darling)have'—100. 'luminous tendril of celestial wish'.

B

Contributions to Periodicals

NOTE: Periodicals are arranged chronologically. Titles of poems are printed in SMALL CAPITAL letters.

A group of early poems, printed in Boston newspapers around the turn of the century, and a contribution to an anniversary issue of a Jewish community paper, published on the West Coast and dated about 1940, are the only known omissions in this section. An exhaustive search has failed to uncover any clue to their whereabouts.

B

Contributions to Periodicals

B1 VISION. *The Harvard Monthly*, LIII. 2 (November 1911), 43.
  First line: 'The dim deep of a yellow evening slides'.

B2 [TWO POEMS]. *The Harvard Monthly*, LV. 5 (February 1913), 170.
  Contents: MIST ('Earth is become the seat of a new sea;')—
  WATER-LILIES ('Behold—a mere like a madonna's head').

B3 MUSIC. *The Harvard Monthly*, LVI. 1 (March 1913), 11.
  First line: 'Music is sweet from the thrush's throat!'.

B4 SUMMER SILENCE (SPENSERIAN STANZA). *The Harvard Advocate*, XCV.
  1 (March 7, 1913), 14.
  First line: 'Eruptive lightnings flutter to and fro'.

B5 SUNSET. *The Harvard Advocate*, XCV. 2 (March 21, 1913), 16.
  First line: 'Great carnal mountains crouching in the cloud'.

B6 OF NICOLETTE. *The Harvard Advocate*, XCV. 2 (March 21, 1913),
  25–26.
  First line: 'Dreaming in marble all the palace lay,'.
  Reprinted as 'dreaming in marble all the castle lay'.

B7 BALLADE. *The Harvard Advocate*, XCV. 4 (April 25, 1913), [47].
  First line: 'The white night roared with a huge north-wind,'.

B8 [TWO] SONNETS. *The Harvard Monthly*, LVI. 3 (May 1913), 97.
  Contents: 'A rain-drop on the eyelids of the earth'—'Long since,
  the flicker brushed with shameless wing'.

B9 [POEM]. *The Harvard Monthly*, LVI. 4 (June 1913), 128.
  First line: 'Do you remember when the fluttering dusk,'.

B10 NOCTURNE. *The Harvard Monthly*, LVIII. 1 (March 1914), 18–20.
  First line: 'When the lithe moonlight silently'.

E. E. Cummings

B11 SONNET. *The Harvard Monthly*, LVIII. 3 (May 1914), 79.
First line: 'For that I have forgot the world these days,'.

B12 NIGHT. *The Harvard Monthly*, LIX. 2 (November 1914), 69–70.
First line: 'Night, with sunset hauntings;'.
The page heading for this poem is "Fancies". However, an examination of other issues of the *Monthly* reveals that the word "Fancies" was used as a page heading for several poems of different titles by various authors. It is reasonable to assume that "Fancies" was a department or feature of the magazine and not the title of any one poem that appeared under it.

B13 OUT OF THE BENGALI. *The Harvard Monthly*, LIX. 3 (December 1914), 85.
First line: 'I spoke to thee with a smile'.
Reprinted as ORIENTALE ('i spoke to thee') in *Vanity Fair*, XIX. 1 (September 1922), 45.

B14 SONNET. *The Harvard Monthly*. LIX. 4 (Christmas 1914), 115.
First line: 'No sunset, but a grey, great, struggling sky'.

B15 LONGING. *The Harvard Monthly*, LX. 2 (April 1915), 37–38.
First line: 'I miss you in the dawn, of gradual flowering lights'.

B16 BALLAD OF LOVE. *The Harvard Monthly*, LX. 3 (May 1915), 91–92.
First line: 'Where is my love! I cried.'.

B17 The New Art (Commencement Part). *The Harvard Advocate*, XCIX. 10 (June 24, 1915), [154]–156.

B18 The King. *The Harvard Monthly*, LX. 5 (July 1915), 132–136.

B19 BALLADE OF SOUL. *The Harvard Monthly*, LX. 5 (July 1915), 141–142.
First line: 'Not for the naked make I this my prayer,'.

B20 SAPPHICS. *The Harvard Monthly*, LXI. 4 (January 1916), 101.
First line: 'When my life his pillar has raised to heaven,'.

B21 [TWO POEMS]. *The Harvard Monthly*, LXII. 1 (March 1916), 8–9.
Contents: BALLAD ('All in green went my love riding')—SONNET ('I dreamed I was among the conquerors,').

B22 SONNET. *The Harvard Monthly*, LXII. 2 (April 1916), 34.
First line: 'It may not always be so; and I say'.
Reprinted as 'it may not always be so; and i say'.

B23 HOKKU. *The Harvard Monthly*, LXII. 2 (April 1916), 55.
First line: 'I care not greatly'.

B24 W. H. W., JR. IN MEMORY OF ''A HOUSE OF POMEGRANATES''. *The Harvard Monthly*, LXII. 4 (June 1916), 123.
First line: 'Speak to me friend! Or is the world so wide'.

B25 SEVEN POEMS. *The Dial*, LXVIII. 1 (January 1920), 22–26.
Contents: I. 'little tree'—II. 'the bigness of cannon'—III. 'Buffalo Bill's'—IV. 'when god lets my body be'—V. 'why did you go'—VI. 'when life is quite through with'—VII. 'O Distinct'.

B26 Gaston Lachaise. *The Dial*, LXVIII. 2 (February 1920), [194]–204.
Reprinted, in part, as ''By E. E. Cummings from *The Dial*, Vol. LXVIII, February, 1920'' and ''On Lachaise''.

B27 FIVE POEMS. *The Dial*, LXVIII. 5 (May 1920), [577]–582.
Contents: I. 'into the strenuous briefness'—II. 'O sweet spontaneous'—III. 'but the other'—IV. 'in Just-'—V. 'spring omnipotent goddess Thou'.
Poem ''v'' reprinted as 'spring omnipotent goddess thou dost'.

B28 T. S. Eliot. *The Dial*, LXVIII. 6 (June 1920), [781]–784.
A review of *Poems* (1919) by T. S. Eliot.

B29 PUELLA MEA. *The Dial*, LXX. 1 (January 1921), [48]–54.
First line: 'Harun Omar and Master Hafiz'.
Lines 181–220 of the *Tulips and Chimneys'* version of this poem are not to be found in this first appearance.

B30 MAISON. *The Liberator*, IV. 7 (July 1921), 24.
First line: 'My love is building a building'.
Reprinted as 'my love is building a building'.

B31 LIBATION. *The Liberator*, IV. 7 (July 1921), 34.
First line: 'O Thou to whom the musical white spring'.

B32 POEM. *The Dial*, LXXI. 4 (October 1921), [439]–440.
First line: 'Always before your voice my soul'.
The final verse paragraph, beginning 'The flute of morning stilled in noon—', was reprinted as TWILIGHT in *Vanity Fair*, XXII. 1 (March 1924), 47.

B33 FIVE POEMS. *The Dial*, LXXII. 1 (January 1922), [43]–46.
Contents: I. 'of evident invisibles'—II. 'conversation with my friend is particularly'—III. 'it is at moments after i have dreamed'—IV. 'by little accurate saints thickly which tread'—V. 'who's most afraid of death? thou'.

B34 POEM. *The Dial*, LXXII. 4 (April 1922), [354]–355.
First line: 'at the head of this street a gasping organ is waving motheaten'.

B35 THREE UNITED STATES SONNETS. *Broom*, II. 2 (May 1922), 146–147.

E. E. Cummings

Contents: I. 'when you rang at Dick Mid's place'—II. 'the Cambridge ladies who live in furnished souls'—III. 'by god i want above fourteenth'.

Poem "I" reprinted as 'when you rang at Dick Mid's Place.'

B36 SUNSET. *Broom*, II. 4 (July 1922), 273.
First line: 'stinging'.

B37 THREE PORTRAITS. *Broom*, II. 4 (July 1922), 306–308.
Contents: I. PIANIST ('ta')—II. CARITAS ('the skinny voice')—III. ARTHUR WILSON ('as usual i did not find him in cafes, the more dissolute').

B38 FOUR POEMS. *Secession*, no. 2 (July 1922), [1]–4.
Contents: I. 'on the Madam's best april the'—II. '(and i imagine' —III. 'life hurl my'—IV. 'workingman with hand so hairy-sturdy'.

B39 POEM, OR BEAUTY HURTS MR. VINAL. *S·4·N*, Issue 23, Year 4 (December 1922), [*unpaged*].
First line: 'take it from me kiddo'.

B40 [ELEVEN] POEMS. *Vanity Fair*, XIX. 4 (December 1922), 67, 116.
Contents: I. ORIENTALE ('my love')—II. 'i like'—III. 'i will wade out/ till my thighs are steeped in burning flowers'—IV. 'goodby Betty, don't remember me'—V. 'ladies and gentlemen this little girl'—VI. AMORES ('if i believe')—VII. 'cruelly, love'—VIII. 'consider O'—IX. 'Where's Madge then,'—X. 'as is the sea marvelous'—XI. 'Lady of Silence'.

B41 SEVEN POEMS. *The Dial*, LXXIV. 1 (January 1923), [25]–30.
Contents: I. 'suppose'—II. 'at dusk/ just when'—III. 'before the fragile gradual throne of night'—IV. 'Take for example this:' —V. 'of this sunset(which is so'—VI. 'Paris; this April sunset completely utters'—VII. 'will out of the kindness of their hearts a few philosophers tell me'.

B42 [THREE] POEMS. *The Little Review*, IX. 3 (Spring 1923), 22–24.
Contents: I. 'because// an obstreporous grin minutely floats' —II. 'said John Roosevelt'—III. 'listen// this a dog barks and'.
Poem "II" reprinted, with a completely revised text, as 'remarked Robinson Jefferson'.

B43 [TWO POEMS]. *The Chapbook*, no. 36 (April 1923), 7–9.
Contents: I. 'but observe; although'—II. 'nobody loses all the time'.

B44 FOUR POEMS. *Secession*, no. 5 (July 1923), 13–17.
Contents: I. 'a man who had fallen among thieves'—II. 'poets

yeggs and thirsties'—III. 'the season 'tis, my lovely lambs,'—IV. 'this evangelist'.

B45 FIVE AMERICANS. *Broom*, v. 3 (October 1923), 134–136.
  Contents: I. LIZ ('with breathing as (faithfully) her lownecked') —II. MAME ('she puts down the handmirror. ''Look at'' arranging')—III. GERT ('joggle i think will do it although the glad') —IV. MARJ ('''life?/ Listen'' the feline she with radishred') —V. FRAN ('should i entirely ask of god why').

B46 FOUR POEMS. *Broom*, v. 4 (November 1923), 204–207.
  Contents: I. 'when the spent day begins to frail'—II. 'my small-headed pearshaped'—III. 'now that fierce few'—IV. 'the wind is a Lady with'.

B47 FOUR SONNETS IN THE MODERNIST MANNER. *Vanity Fair*, XXI. 4 (December 1923), 60.
  Contents: I. 'touching you i say (it being Spring'—II. 'if i have made, my lady, intricate'—III. 'after all white horses are in bed' —IV. 'our touching hearts slenderly comprehend'.

B48 FOUR POEMS. *Broom*, VI. 1 (January 1924), 1–5.
  Contents: I. 'ohld song'—2. 'i'd think ''wonder'—3. 'if (you are i why certainly'—4. 'Will i ever forget that precarious moment?'.

B49 FOUR POEMS. *The Dial*, LXXVI. 1 (January 1924), [29]–32.
  Contents: I. 'O Thou to whom the musical white spring'—II. 'perhaps it is to feel strike'—III. 'Picasso'—IV. 'at the ferocious phenomenon of 5 o'clock i find myself gently de-'.

B50 FOUR POEMS. *the transatlantic review*, I. 1 (January 1924), 1–5.
  Contents: I. 'impossibly'—II. 'voices to voices, lip to lip'—III. 'death is more than'—IV. 'weazened Irrefutable unastonished'.

B51 THREE POEMS. *1924*, no. 2 (August 1924), 36–38.
  Contents: I. 'it is winter a moon in the afternoon'—II. 'why are these pipples taking their hets off?'—III. 'sunlight was over'.

B52 The Soul Story of Gladys Vanderdecker. *Vanity Fair*, XXIII. 4 (December 1924), 52, 92, 94, 114.
  Signed: The Society Editor of Vanity Fair.

B53 Vanity Fair's Prize Movie-Scenario. *Vanity Fair*, XXIII. 5 (January 1925), 51, 90.
  Signed: C. E. Niltse, A Master of Screen Continuity.

B54 What Our Loving Subscribers Say. *Vanity Fair*, XXIII. 6 (February 1925), 57. Unsigned.

E. E. Cummings

B55 MEMORABILIA. *Vanity Fair*, XXIV. 1 (March 1925), 30.
First line: 'stop look &'.

B56 An Ex-Multimillionaire's Rules for Success in Life. *Vanity Fair*, XXIV. 1 (March 1925), 32, 98. Photograph by Florence Vandamm.
Signed: C. E. Niltse, Success Editor of Vanity Fair.

B57 A Modern Gulliver Explores the Movies. *Vanity Fair*, XXIV. 1 (March 1925), 49, 106, 108. Photograph by Sarony.
Signed: Sir Arthur Catchpole, Bart., D.C.L., K.C.B., R.S.V.P., etc.

B58 When Calvin Coolidge Laughed. *Vanity Fair*, XXIV. 2 (April 1925), 52, 98.
Reprinted, with revisions, as "Chapter I" of [*no title*].

B59 William Adams-Wiggley: Genius and Christian. *Vanity Fair*, XXIV. 2 (April 1925), 59, 88, 92, 106.
Signed: C. E. Niltse, S.P.C.V.

B60 THREE POEMS. *Vanity Fair*, XXIV. 3 (May 1925), 44.
Contents: PATRIOT ('"next to of course god america i')—ITEM ('this man is o so')—ODE ('o// the sweet & aged people').

B61 Seven Samples of Dramatic Criticism. *Vanity Fair*, XXIV. 3 (May 1925), 58.

B62 Unexpected Light on the Dawes Plan. *Vanity Fair*, XXIV. 3 (May 1925), 69, 92.
Signed: N. G. Archibald, Ph.D., L.L.D.

B63 Jean Cocteau as a Graphic Artist. *Vanity Fair*, XXV. 1 (September 1925), 46, 94. Drawings by Jean Cocteau.

B64 How to Succeed as an Author. *Vanity Fair*, XXV. 1 (September 1925), 60.
Signed: Scribner Tickel, Author of: "Can Spring Be Far Behind".

B65 A POEM. *The Dial*, LXXIX. 4 (October 1925), [304].
First line: 'Nobody wears a yellow'.

B66 The Adult, the Artist and the Circus. *Vanity Fair*, XXV. 2 (October 1925), 57, 98. Painting by George Bellows.

B67 The Very Latest School in Art. *Vanity Fair*, XXV. 2 (October 1925), 65, 94.
Signed: Scribner Tickel.

B68 Everybody's Mother, Anybody's Mate. *Vanity Fair*, XXV. 2 (October 1925), 75. Drawing by Frans Masereel.
Signed: An Anonymous Author.

B : Periodicals

B69 Helen Whiffletree, American Poetess. *Vanity Fair*, xxv. 3 (November 1925), 64, 114.
Signed: P. H. Dunkels, N.G.

B70 You Aren't Mad, Am I? *Vanity Fair*, xxv. 4 (December 1925), 73, 92. Three line drawings—"The Jew Comedian", "Cleo" and "Dance du Ventre"—by the author.

B71 FOUR POEMS. *The Dial*, LXXX. 1 (January 1926), [17]–20.
Contents: I. 'i go to this window'—II. 'if being morticed with a dream'—III. 'how this uncouth enchanted'—IV. 'but if i should say'.

B72 "I Confess!" *Vanity Fair*, xxv. 5 (January 1926), 63, 92. Illustrated with "sex" magazine covers.
Signed: John F. Rutter.

B73 "I Take Great Pleasure In Presenting". *Vanity Fair*, xxv. 6 (February 1926), 57, 78. Photographs by Florence Vandamm.

B74 Little Red Riding Hood. *Vanity Fair*, xxvi. 1 (March 1926), 75, 126. Drawing by Benito.
Signed: Eugene Heltai.

B75 POEM. *The Dial*, LXXX. 4 (April 1926), 300.
First line: 'supposing that i dreamed this)'.
Reprinted as 'supposing i dreamed this)'.

B76 The Theatre. *The Dial*, LXXX. 4 (April 1926), [343]–345.
A review of The Moscow Art Theatre Musical Studio. Reprinted as "The Theatre: I".

B77 The Theatre. *The Dial*, LXXX. 5 (May 1926), [432]–435.
Reviews of *Little Eyolf*, The International Theatre Exposition and the Greb-Flowers middleweight fight. Reprinted as "The Theatre: II".

B78 Coney Island. *Vanity Fair*, xxvi. 4 (June 1926), 66, 130. Drawing Frans Masereel.

B79 Conflicting Aspects of Paris. *Vanity Fair*, xxvi. 6 (August 1926), 65, 82. Etching by Edouard Goerg.

B80 Vive la Folie! *Vanity Fair*, xxvii. 1 (September 1926), 55, 116. Painting by Bernheim Jeune.

B81 How I Do Not Love Italy. *Vanity Fair*, xxvii. 2 (October 1926), 60, 122. Illustrated with a photograph of Benito Mussolini.

B82 The Tabloid Newspaper. *Vanity Fair*, xxvii. 4 (December 1926), 83, 146. Illustrated with front pages from the New York *Evening Graphic*.

E. E. Cummings

B83 Frenzied Finance. *Vanity Fair*, xxvii. 5 (Januarv 1927), 41, 90. Drawing by Frans Masereel.

B84 The Secret of the Zoo Exposed. *Vanity Fair*, xxviii. 1 (March 1927), 66-67. Woodcuts by Leon Underwood.

B85 Ivan Narb: Abstract Sculptor of the Cosmic. *Vanity Fair*, xxviii. 1 (March 1927), 76, 115. Illustrated with two unsigned drawings. *Signed:* Gwendolyn Orloff.

B86 The Agony of the Artist (With a Capital A). *Vanity Fair*, xxviii. 2 (April 1927), 68, 98.

B87 Why I Like America. *Vanity Fair*, xxviii. 3 (May 1927), 61, 110. Drawing—"La 'Beauté' Francaise"—by the author.

B88 Him. *The Dial*, lxxxiii. 2 (August 1927), [101]-127.
All or part of Act I, Scene II, Act II, Scene VI, and Act III, Scenes I, V, VI, and VII of the finished play.

B89 The New Mother Goose. *Vanity Fair*, xxviii. 6 (August 1927), 65, 82.

B90 Mr. X. *The Bookman*, lxvi. 1 (September 1927), 39-41.

B91 Miracles and Dreams. *Cinema*, i. 5 (June 1930), 14, 55. Illustrated with drawings of animated cartoon characters.

B92 TWO POEMS. *This Quarter*, iii. 3 (March 1931), 473-474.
Contents: 1. 'come a little further—why be afraid—'—2. 'if there are heavens my mother will(all by herself)have'.
Poem "2" reprinted as 'if there are any heavens my mother will(all by herself)have'.

B93 THREE POEMS. *This Quarter*, iii. 4 (June 1931), 599-601.
Contents: 1. 'When rain whom fear'—ii. 'i met a man under the moon'—iii. 'you'.
Poem "1" reprinted as 'when rain whom fear'.

B94 TWO POEMS. *Hound & Horn*, iv. 4 (July/September 1931), 569-570.
Contents: 'so standing,our eyes filled with wind,and the'— 'somewhere i have never travelled,gladly beyond'.

B95 SIX POEMS. *Pagany*, ii. 3 (Summer 1931), 58-61.
Contents: i. 'come a little further—why be afraid—'—ii. 'if i love You'—iii. 'speaking of love(of'—iv. 'lady will you come with me into'—v. 'somewhere i have never travelled,gladly beyond'—vi. 'my darling since'.

B96 THE RED FRONT—L. Aragon. Translated from the French by E. E. Cummings. *Literature of the World Revolution*, no. 3 (August 1931), [35]-42.

First line: 'A gentleness for my dog'.

Reprinted, with corrections, in *Contempo*, III. 5 (February 1, 1933), 4–5, 8.

B97 THREE POEMS. *This Quarter*, IV. 1 (September 1931), 11–13.

Contents: 1. 'what time is it i wonder never mind'—II. 'in a middle of a room'—III. 'i will cultivate within'.

B98 TWO POEMS. *This Quarter*, IV. 2 (December 1931), 252–253.

Contents: 1. 'nothing is more exactly terrible than'—II. 'Wing Wong,uninterred at twice'.

A first printing of an early version of poem "1". Both poems first appeared in *ViVa*.

B99 FOUR POEMS. *Contact*, I. 1 (February 1932), [10]–13.

Contents: 1. '"let's start a magazine'—2. 'r-p-o-p-h-e-s-s-a-g-r'—3. 'mouse)Won'—4. 'ondumonde'.

B100 From a Russian Diary. *Hound & Horn*, v. 3 (April/June 1932), [364]–406.

"Sun. 10", "Monday, 11 May" and "Tues." as published in *Eimi*, pp. 3–34.

B101 A Fairy Tale. New York *Evening Journal*, no. 16,485 (Friday, July 15, 1932), 13.

Gilbert Seldes' column "True to Type" is devoted to a contribution by Cummings titled as above.

B102 The Tomb of Lenin. *Hound & Horn*, VI. 1 (October/December 1932), [20]–60.

"Sat., 16 mai" and "Sat. 30th mai" as published in *Eimi*, pp. 73–88, 232–246.

B103 And It Came To Pass. *Americana*, I. 1 (November 1932), 3–4. Unsigned drawings by Alexander King.

B104 BALLAD OF AN INTELLECTUAL. *Americana*, I. 2 (December 1932), 11.

First line: 'Listen, you morons great and small'.

B105 Weligion Is Hashish. *Americana*, I. 3 (January 1933), 26. Unsigned drawing.

B106 [Letter to the Editors]. *Contempo*, III. 6 (February 21, 1933), 2.

The author's reaction to his publishers calling *Eimi* a novel. A reply from Pascal Covici, the publisher, appeared in *Contempo*, III. 11 (July 25, 1933), 2.

B107 In Memoriam. *Americana*, I. 5 (March 1933), 8. Illustrated with a photograph of penguins.

B108 POEM. *American Poetry Journal*, June 1934, 29.

First line: 'Spring(side'.

E. E. Cummings

B109 SIX POEMS. *Hound & Horn*, VII. 4 (July/September 1934), [582]–586.
    Contents: I. 'reason let others flaunt and realness wear—'
—II. 'death(having lost)put on his universe'—III. 'out of a
supermetamathical subpreincestures'—IV. 'how dark and single,
where he ends,the earth'—V. 'the(/Wistfully'—VI. 'does
yesterday's perfection seem not quite'.
    Poem "I" reprinted as 'reason let others give and realness
bring—'.

B110 [Answers to] An Enquiry. *New Verse*, no. 11 (October 1934),
10–11.
    Quotations from *Him, Eimi, The Enormous Room* and the "Fore-
word" to *Is 5* arranged as answers to six questions.

B111 [NINE POEMS]. *Alcestis*, I. 2 (January 1935), [*unpaged*].
    Contents: I. 'jehovah buried,satan dead,'—II. 'a)glazed mind
layed in a/ urinal'—III. 'when muckers pimps and tratesmen'
—IV. 'this little'—V. 'What does little Ernest croon'—VI.
'kumrads die because they're told)'—VII. 'worshipping Same'—
VIII. 'come(all you mischief-'—IX. 'conceive a man,should he
have anything'.
    Poems "I", "V" and "IX" were reprinted as THREE POEMS
(I. 'conceive a man,should he have anything'—II. 'Jehovah
buried,Satan dead,'—III. 'what does little Ernest croon') in
The New English Weekly, VII. 17 (February 7, 1935), 351.

B112 FIVE POEMS. *Esquire*, III. 5 (May 1935), 39. Sketches by John Groth.
    Contents: I. 'that which we who're alive in spite of mirrors'
—II. 'sh estiffl'—III. 'o// sure)but'—IV. 'sonnet entitled how
to run the world'—V. 'IN)/all those who got'.
    An editorial note in "Backstage with Esquire", p. 22B, reads:
". . . these five poems appear in [Cummings'] new book, *No
Thanks*, which was scheduled for publication on April first but
postponed to give us time to come out with this selection."

B113 Exit the Boob. *Esquire*, III. 6 (June 1935), 33, 155. Illustrated
with a photograph of a sculpture in clay by Eric Lundgren.

B114 Burlesque—I Love It! *Stage*, XII. 6 (March 1936), 61. Drawing on
p. 60—"New York Audiences No. IV, The Irving Place Burlesque"—by Alexander King.

B115 POEM. *Contemporary Poetry and Prose*, no. 1 (May 1936), 4–5.
    First line: '(of Ever-Ever Land i speak'.

B116 THREE POEMS. *Townsman*, I. 1 (January 1938), 2–3.
    Contents: I. 'The Mind's('—II. 'american critic ad 1935'—III.
'hanged'.

B : Periodicals

B117 Speech from a Forthcoming Play. *Partisan Review*, IV. 4 (March 1938), 22–23.
Reprinted as "Speech: II".

B118 Fair Warning. *Junior League Magazine*, XXIV. 9 (May 1938), 40.

B119 What About It? *Twice A Year*, I (Fall/Winter 1938), 138–142.

B120 SEVEN POEMS. *Poetry* (Chicago), LIII. 4 (January 1939), 169–175.
Contents I. 'mortals)'—II. 'these children singing in stone a'—III. 'nouns to nouns'—IV. ')when what hugs stopping earth than silent is'—V. 'up into the silence the green'—VI. 'six'—VII. 'love is more thicker than forget'.

B121 DIRGE. *Furioso*, I. 1 (Summer 1939), 13.
First line: 'flotsam and jetsam'.

B122 POEM. *Poetry World*, X. 12/XI. 1 (July/August 1939), 13.
First line: 'spoke joe to jack'.

B123 SONNET. *Furioso*, I. 2 (New Year 1940), 18.
First line: 'there are possibly 2½ or impossibly 3'.

B124 THREE POEMS. *Furioso*, I. 3 (Spring 1940), 24–25.
Contents: One. '!blac'—Two. 'these people socalled were not given hearts'—Three. 'one slipslouch twi'.

B125 [A Letter to the Editors in] War Writers on Democracy. *Life*, VIII. 26 (June 24, 1940), 12.

B126 FIVE POEMS. *Poetry* (Chicago), LVI. 5 (August 1940), 233–239.
Contents: I. 'anyone lived in a pretty how town'—II. 'you which could grin three smiles into a dead'—III. 'a pretty a day'—IV. 'i say no world'—V. 'If you can't eat you got to'.

B127 Speech from A Play. *Furioso*, I. 4 (Summer 1941), 37–41.
Reprinted as "Speech: III".

B128 FOUR POEMS. *Furioso*, II. 1 (1943), 9–11.
Contents: I. 'when god decided to invent'—2. 'it's over a(see just'—3. 'life is more true than reason will deceive'—4. 'if(among'.

B129 EIGHT POEMS. *View*, Series III. 2 (June 1943), 53.
Contents: I. 'old mr ly'—2. 'applaws)'—3. 'a salesman is an it that stinks Excuse'—4. 'a politician is an arse upon'—5. 'ygUDuh'—6. 'mr u will not be missed'—7. 'pity this busy monster,manunkind,'—8. 'darling!because my blood can sing'.

B130 FIVE POEMS. *Poetry* (Chicago), LXII.4 (July 1943), 179–184.
Contents: I. 'one's not half two. It's two are halves of one:'—II. 'what if a much of a which of a wind'—III. 'rain or hail'—IV.

'might these be thrushes climbing through almost(do they'—v. 'if everything happen that can't be done'.

Poem "II" reprinted as WHAT IF A MUCH in *Harper's Bazaar*, LXXVII. 2781 (September 1943), 168.

B131 THREE POEMS. *Accent*, III. 4 (Summer 1943), 228–229.

Contents: 1. 'Hello is what a mirror says'—2. 'life is more true than reason will deceive'—3. 'o by the by'.

B132 POEM. *Quarterly Review of Literature*, I. 1 (Autumn 1943), 3.

First line: 'of all the blessings which to man'.

B133 POEM. *Accent*, IV. 2 (Winter 1944), 100.

First line: 'it was a goodly co'.

B134 POEM. *Maryland Quarterly*, no. 3 (Summer 1944), 116.

First line: 'o to be in finland'.

Part of a letter to the Editors that accompanied the poem is printed in "Notes", p. 176.

B135 ["Is Something Wrong?" in] War and the Poets (A Symposium), edited by Oscar Williams. *Harper's Magazine*, CXC. 1139 (April 1945), 464–465.

B136 [FIVE POEMS]. *Circle*, no. 5 (Spring 1945), 14–15.

Contents: 1. 'out of more find than seeks'—2. 'this out of within itself moo'—3. 'one day a nigger'—4. 'blossoming are people'—5. 'honour corruption villainy holiness'.

B137 POEM. *The Harvard Wake*, I. 4 (June 1945), 10.

First line: 'when an honest injun toma'.

Reprinted as 'when your honest redskin toma'.

B138 POEM. *Pacific*, I. 1 (November 1945), 9.

First line: 'who were so dark of heart they might not speak,'.

B139 ["Re Ezra Pound" in] The Case of Ezra Pound, by Charles Norman. *PM*, VI. 138 (Sunday, November 25, 1945), m16.

B140 The Old Man who said "Why?" *The Harvard Wake* (Cummings Number), no. 5 (Spring 1946), 5–8.

Reprinted, with decoration by Alfred Russell, in *Mademoiselle*, XXIV. 5 (March 1947), [208]–[209], 312–314.

B141 POEM. *The Harvard Wake* (Cummings Number), no. 5 (Spring 1946), 9.

First line: 'love our so right'.

B142 Santa Claus (A Morality). *The Harvard Wake* (Cummings Number), no. 5 (Spring 1946), 10–19.

B143 [Part of a Letter to Paul Rosenfeld in] The Voyages, by Paul

B : Periodicals

Rosenfeld. *The Harvard Wake* (Cummings Number), no. 5 (Spring 1946), 35–36.
> A tribute to and description of Cummings' father.

B144 A Foreword to Krazy. *The Sewanee Review*, LIV. 2 (Spring 1946), [216]–221.
> Reprinted as "Introduction".

B145 SEVEN POEMS. *Quarterly Review of Literature*, II. 4 (Spring 1946), [273]–277.
> *Contents:* 1. 'quick i the death of thing'—2. 'F is for foetus(a'—3. 'a kike is the most dangerous'—4. 'where's Jack Was'—5. 'why must itself up every of a park'—6. 'no time ago'—7. '(nothing whichful about'.

B146 FIVE POEMS. *Yale Poetry Review*, II. 1 (Summer 1946), 3–6.
> *Contents:* 1. 'a like a'—2. 'a(ncient)a'—3. 'three wealthy sisters swore they'd never part:'—4. 'maybe god'—5. 'swim so now million many worlds in each'.

B147 [A Statement in] Poets Here Scorn Soviet Attack on Work. New York *Times*, XCVI, 32,490 (Tuesday, January 7, 1947), 25.

B148 FOUR POEMS. *The Ark*, Spring 1947, 40–41.
> *Contents:* One. 'hair your a brook'—Two. 'i'm'—Three. 'out of the mountain of his soul comes'—Four. 'summer is over'.

B149 SEVEN POEMS. *Poetry* (Chicago), LXX. 6 (September 1947), 293–299.
> *Contents:* 1. 'this(let's remember)day died again and'—2. 'neither awake'—3. 'infinite jukethrob smoke & swallow to dis'—4. 'jake hates/ all the girls(the'—5. 'whose are these (wraith a clinging with a wraith)'—6. 'this is a rubbish of human rind'—7. 'if(touched by love's own secret)we,like homing'.

B150 POEM. *Horizon*, no. 93/94 (October 1947), 67.
> *First line:* 'to start,to hesitate;to stop'.

B151 [POEM]. *Epoch*, I. 1 (Fall 1947), 21–22.
> *First line:* 'goo-dmore-ning(en'.

B152 POEM. *Cronos*, I. 3 (Fall 1947), 4.
> *First line:* '(swooming)a pillar of youngly'.

B153 POEM. *Halcyon*, I. 1 (Winter 1948), 51.
> *First line:* 'i thank you God for most this amazing'.
> Reprinted as 'i thank You God for most this amazing'.

B154 Concerning Art. *Berkeley*, no. 2 (1948), 1–2. Two oil paintings —"Self Portrait" and "The Brooksday Farm"—by the author.
> *Contents:* [Foreword to *CIOPW*]—["Foreword" to the Ameri-

E. E. Cummings

can British Art Center catalogue, 1944]—["foreword" to the Rochester Memorial Gallery catalogue, 1945]—["Re Ezra Pound"].

B155 POEM. *Berkeley*, no. 2 (1948), 2.
First line: 'the of an it ignoblest he'.

B156 POEM. *The Hudson Review*, I. 1 (Spring 1948), [96].
First line: ' &(all during the'.

B157 A Little Girl Named I. *Wake*, no. 6 (Spring 1948), 3–5.

B158 POEM. *Botteghe Oscure*, no. 2 (Autumn 1948), 279.
First line: 'when faces called flowers float out of the ground'.

B159 SIX POEMS. *Quarterly Review of Literature*, IV. 3 (Autumn 1948), 238–241.
Contents: 1. 'pieces(in darker'—2. 'when serpents bargain for the right to squirm'—3. 'blue the triangular why'—4. 'so many selves(so many fiends and gods'—5. 'if the'—6. 'luminous tendril of celestial wish'.

B160 On Art. *Twice A Year* (10th Anniversary Issue), no. XIV/XV (1948), 301–303.
Contents: 1. Foreword to Catalogue for an Exhibition of Cummings' Paintings [at the American British Art Center, 1944]—II. On Lachaise.

B161 FIVE POEMS. *Partisan Review*, XVI. 2 (February 1949), 152–155.
Contents: 1. 'tw'—2. 'noone" autumnal this great lady's gaze'—3. 'chas sing does(who'—4. 'dying is fine)but Death'— 5. 'we miss you,jack—tactfully you(with one cocked'.

B162 PORTRAIT. *Voices*, no. 137 (Spring 1949), 18.
First line: 'after screamgroa'.

B163 Words into Pictures. *Art News*, XLVIII. 3 (May 1949), 15. Two oil paintings—"Self-portrait" and "Portrait in Shadow"—by the author.
The piece is accompanied by a brief appreciation of Cummings' American British Art Center exhibit (1949) by "T.B.H.".

B164 Eleven Quotations. *Poetry* (Chicago), LXXIV. 2 (May 1949), 91–93.
A letter to the Editors with quotations from *Letters to a Young Poet*, by Rainer Maria Rilke.

B165 SEVEN POEMS. *Poetry* (Chicago), LXXIV. 4 (July 1949), 187–193.
Contents: 1. 'if a cheerfulest Elephantangelchild should sit'—II. 'a thrown a'—III. 'open his head,baby'—IV. 'possibly thrice we glimpsed—/more likely twice'—V. '(im)c-a-t(mo)'—VI.

'in// Spring comes(no-'—vII. 'now all the fingers of this tree(darling)have'.

B166 POEM. *Poetry Ireland*, no. 7 (October 1949), 17.
First line: 'who sharpens every dull'.

B167 POEM. *Wake*, no. 8 (Autumn 1949), 4.
First line: 'stand with your lover on the ending earth—'.

B168 POEM. *Shenandoah*, I. 3 (Winter 1950), 23.
First line: '"nothing" the unjust man complained'.

B169 POEM. *The University of Kansas City Review*, XVI. 3 (Spring 1950), 161.
First line: 'first robin the;'.

B170 POEM. *Imagi*, no. 13—v. 2 (Spring 1950), 11.
First line: 'whatever's merely wilful,'.

B171 POEM. *The Hopkins Review*, III. 4 (Summer 1950), 17.
First line: 'round a so moon could dream(i sus'.

B172 POEM. *Montevallo Review*, Summer 1950, 8.
First line: 'old age sticks'.

B173 SEVEN POEMS. *Poetry* (Chicago), LXXVI. 4 (July 1950), 187–193.
Contents: 1. 'dim'—2. 'spirit colossal'—3. 'jack's white horse(up'—4. '!'—5. 'if the Lovestar grows most big'—6. 'crazy jay blue)'—7. 'if up's the word;and a world grows greener'.

B174 POEM. *Spearhead*, II. 1 (Summer 1950), [13].
First line: 'ev erythingex Cept:'.
Reprinted in *Shenandoah*, II. 3 (Winter 1951), 29.

B175 POEM. *Accent*, x. 4 (Autumn 1950), 224.
First line: 'being to timelessness as it's to time,'.
Reprinted in *The Times Literary Supplement*, 53rd Year, no. 2746 (Friday, September 17, 1954), liv.

B176 POEM. *Gryphon*, no. 2 (Fall 1950), 11.
First line: 'Young m'.

B177 The House that Ate Mosquito Pie. *Wake*, no. 9 (Autumn 1950), 5–7.

B178 POEM. *Kavita* (Calcutta), XVI. 1 (December 1950), [1].
First line: 'how generous is that himself the sun'.

B179 SONG. *diameter*, no. 1 (March 1951), [41].
First line: 'now(more near ourselves than we)'.
Reprinted in *Music & Letters*, XXXII. 3 (July 1951), 251.

B180 [A Letter to the Editor]. *The Explicator*, IX. 5 (March 1951), [*unpaged*].

E. E. Cummings

The author's reaction to Richard B. Vowles' explication of 'Space being(don't forget to remember)Curved' in *The Explicator*, IX. I (October 1950), [*unpaged*].

B181 FOR MARION. *Experiment*, V. 4 (Spring 1951), 412.
First line: 'your birthday comes to tell me this'.
This issue is mistakenly dated "1950".

B182 POEM. *Spearhead*, II. 2 (Spring 1951), 5.
First line: 'seeker of truth'.

B183 Jottings. *Wake*, no. 10 (Spring 1951), 81–83.

B184 POEM. *The Hopkins Review*, IV. 4 (Summer 1951), [41].
First line: 'this man's heart'.

B185 [A Statement in] Authors and Humanism, a classification of Humanism, and statements, by Warren Allen Smith. *The Humanist*, XI. 5 (October/November 1951), 200.

B186 SEVEN POEMS. *Botteghe Oscure*, IX (Spring 1952), 219–223.
Contents: 'lily has a rose'—'albutnotquitemost'—'off a pane)the'—'as joe gould says in'—'home means that'—'So shy shy shy(and with a'—'now what were motionless move (exists no'.

B187 POEM. *dimensions*, Spring 1952, 1.
First line: 'ardensteil-henarub-izabeth)'.

B188 FIVE POEMS. *Poetry* (Chicago), LXXX. 3 (June 1952), 125–129.
Contents: 'dive for dreams'—'all nearness pauses,while a star can grow'—'unlove's the heavenless hell and homeless home'—'i carry your heart with me(i carry it in'—'spring!may—'.

B189 POEM. *Gambit*, I. 3 (September/October 1952), 10.
First line: 'a he as o'.

B190 [POEM]. *The Poet* (Glasgow, Scotland), no. 4 (Autumn 1952), [*unpaged*].
First line: 'that melancholy'.

B191 POEM. *Shenandoah*, III. 3 (Autumn 1952), [29].
First line: 'n'.

B192 POEM. *Poetry* (Chicago), LXXXI. I (October 1952), 20–22.
First line: 'rosetree,rosetree'.

B193 i & my parents' son. *The Atlantic Monthly*, CXCI. 4 (April 1953), 57–62.
Reprinted as "i & their son", the second of *i: Six Nonlectures*.

B194 i & self-discovery. *The Atlantic Monthly*, CXCI. 5 (May 1953), 53–58.
The third of *i: Six Nonlectures*.

B : Periodicals

B195 POEM. *Hobart Review*, IV. 1 (May 1953), 25.
First line: 'the(oo)is'.

B196 FIVE POEMS. *Quarterly Review of Literature*, VII. 2 (Spring 1953), [87]–90.
Contents: 1. 'once White&Gold'—2. 'who(is?are)who'—3. 'handsome and clever and he went cruising'—4. 'you no'—5. 'here's s'.

B197 [Selections from *i: Six Nonlectures* in] The Discovery of Me: E. E. Cummings Reflects on a Year at Harvard as Norton Professor, by Martha Miller. *Harvard Alumni Bulletin*, LV. 15 (May 9, 1953), 610–614, 633.

B198 i & my parents. *New Republic*, CXXIX. 14 (November 2, 1953), 15–17.
An abridged version of the first of *i: Six Nonlectures*.

B199 POEM. *Folio*, XX. 1 (Winter 1954), 26.
First line: 'in time's a noble mercy of proportion'.

B200 ADHUC SUB JUDICE LIS. *New Ventures*, no. 1 (June 1954), 79.
First line: 'when mack smacked phyllis on the snout'.

B201 [A "Communication" about Dylan Thomas]. *The Yale Literary Magazine* (Dylan Thomas Number), CXXII. 2 (November 1954), 19.

B202 POEM. *Pennsylvania Literary Review*, V. 1 (Autumn 1954), 18.
First line: '"but why should"'.

B203 Videlicet. *Arts Digest*, XXIX. 5 (December 1, 1954), 6. Oil painting—"Sea" 1944—by the author.
This issue also contains "E. E. Cummings' Paintings and Poems", by William Carlos Williams. It is illustrated with three works by Cummings: "Charlie Chaplin, 1924" (drawing), "Sunset, 1950" (watercolor), and "Self-Portrait, 1947" (oil).

B204 [A Letter to Karl Shapiro, Editor]. *Poetry* (Chicago), LXXXV. 5 (February 1955), [*inside front cover*].
A letter in support of *Poetry's* drive for financial aid.

B205 POEM. *Accent*, XV. 1 (Winter 1955), 27–28.
First line: '—laughing to find'.

B206 [A Letter to the Drama Editor in] Drama Mailbag—Three Tributes to the Memory of M. Eleanor Fitzgerald. New York *Times*, CIV. 35,505—Section 2 (Sunday, April 10, 1955), 3.

B207 POEM. *Chicago Review*, IX. 2 (Summer 1955), 72.
First line: 'someone i am wandering a town(if its'.

E. E. Cummings

B208 POEM. *New World Writing*, no. 8 (October 1955), 48.
First line: 'let's,from some loud unworld's most rightful wrong'.

B209 Poet Gives Advice to Ottawa Students. *Ottawa Hills Spectator* (Grand Rapids, Michigan), xxx. 2 (October 26, 1955), 2.
Reprinted as "A Poet's Advice to Students".

B210 For Niccolo Tucci. *the village Voice*, 1. 10 (December 28, 1955), 4.
A Christmas greeting to the author of "The Press of Freedom" a column in the *Voice*.

B211 POEM. *Poetry London-New York*, 1. 1 (March/April 1956), 19.
First line: 'over us if(as what was dusk becomes'.

B212 POEM. *PAX*, no. 2 (November 1956), [2].
First line: '(hills chime with thrush)'.

B213 THREE POEMS. *Poetry London-New York*, 1. 2 (Winter 1956), 19–20.
Contents: I. 'who(at'—II. 'both eaching come ghostlike'—III. 'this'.

B214 CHRISTMAS POEM. *The Atlantic Monthly*, cxcviii. 6 (December 1956), 55.
First line: 'from spiralling ecstatically this'.

B215 POEM. *The Colorado Review*, 1. 1 (Winter 1956/1957), 13.
First line: 'maggie and milly and molly and may'.
Reprinted in *the village Voice*, ii. 13 (Wednesday, January 23, 1957), 4, and in the "Poets' Column", *The New York Times Book Review*, lxii. 12 (Sunday, March 24, 1957), 2.

B216 SEVEN POEMS. *Quarterly Review of Literature*, ix, 1 (Spring 1957), [19]–23.
Contents: 'a total stranger one black day'—'what Got him was Noth'—'these from my mother's greatgrandmother's rosebush white'—THANKSGIVING (1956) ('a monstering horror swallows')—'because you take life in your stride(instead'—'dominic has'—'out of the lie of no'.

B217 POEM. *The University of Connecticut Fine Arts Festival Magazine and Connecticut Writer*, Spring 1957, [1]. Illustrated with a photograph of the author.
First line: 'this little huge'.

B218 POEM. *Encounter*, viii. 6 (June 1957), 28.
First line: 'i am a little church(no great cathedral)'.
Reprinted in "E. E. Cummings Reads New Poem Tonight", Boston *Sunday Herald*, ccxxii. 174 (June 23, 1957), 21, and with the first line as title in *Presbyterian Life*, xi. 9 (May 3, 1958), [2].

B : Periodicals

B219 SONG. *The Poet* (Glasgow, Scotland), no. 15 ("Final Issue", Summer 1957), [*unpaged*].
First line: 'but we've the may'.

B220 POEM. *The Literary Review*, I. 1 (Autumn 1957), 74.
First line: 'to stand(alone)in some'.

B221 POEM. *New York Review*, I. 1 (Spring 1958), 5.
First line: 'l(a'.

B222 POEM. *Pennsylvania Literary Review*, VIII. 3 (Spring 1958), 3.
First line: 'i love you much(most beautiful darling)'.

B223 POEM. *The Stylus*, III. 2 (Spring 1958), 3.
First line: 'joyful your complete fearless and pure love'.

B224 POEM. *Accent*, XVIII. 3 (Summer 1958), 157.
First line: 'in time of daffodils(who know'.

B225 POEM. *Compass Review*, no. 3 (Summer 1958), 10.
First line: 'all worlds have halfsight,seeing either with'.

B226 POEM. *San Francisco Review*, I. 1 (Winter 1958), 38.
First line: 'at just 5 a'.

B227 POEM. *Syracuse 10*, I. 2. (December 1958), 19. Illustrated with a sketch of the author from a photograph by Marion Morehouse.
First line: 'D-re-A-mi-N-gl-Y'.

B228 POEM. *Audience*, VI. 1 (Winter 1959), 51.
First line: 'who is this'.

B229 POEM. *Evergreen Review*, II. 8 (Spring 1959), 38.
First line: 'nite)'.

B230 [A Contribution to a Symposium on the Beat Poets in] Comments. *Wagner Literary Magazine*, Spring 1959, 29.

B231 POEM. *The Literary Criterion* (Mysore, India), III. 4 (Summer 1959), [90].
First line: 'all which isn't singing is mere talking'.

B232 POEM. *The Massachusetts Review*, I. 1 (October 1959), 154–155.
First line: 'it's'.

B233 POEM. *The Wormwood Review*, I. 1 (Winter 1960), [*unpaged*].
First line: 'one'.

C

Contributions to Books, Pamphlets, Programs, Catalogues, and a Musical Score

NOTE: Material in this section is arranged chronologically. Titles of poems are printed in SMALL CAPITAL letters.

C

Contributions to Books, Pamphlets, Programs, Catalogues, and a Musical Score

C1 The New Art. In *Secretary's First Report: Harvard College Class of 1915*, [by Malcolm Justin Logan, Class Secretary]. Cambridge, Mass.: Printed for the Class, Crimson Printing Co., May 1916, pp. 217–222.

This reprint of "The New Art (Commencement Part)" is headed "Disquisition" and signed "Edward Estling (sic) Cummings". Also reprinted in *The Harvard Advocate Anthology*, edited by Donald Hall (New York: Twayne Publishers, Inc., 1950), pp. 139–146.

C2 POEM. In *Anthology of Magazine Verse for 1922*, edited by William Stanley Braithwaite. Boston: Small, Maynard & Company, 1923, pp. 58–59.

First line: 'Always before your voice my soul'.

C3 ["Warning": A note to the Provincetown Playhouse production of *Him*]. In *Program*. New York: Provincetown Playhouse, Spring 8363 (i.e. 1928).

C4 [no title]. In *The New American Caravan*, edited by Alfred Kreymborg, Lewis Mumford and Paul Rosenfeld. New York: The Macaulay Company, 1929, pp. 165–183.

C5 Anthropos: or The Future of Art. In *Whither, Whither, or After Sex, What? A Symposium to End Symposiums*, edited by Walter S. Hankel. New York: The Macaulay Company, 1930, pp. 153–165.

C6 Brief Biography. In *Whither, Whither, or After Sex, What? A Symposium to End Symposiums*, edited by Walter S. Hankel. New York: The Macaulay Company, 1930, pp. 165–167.

E. E. Cummings

Signed "Ed." Reprinted in *e. e. cummings and WILLIAM JORGENSEN* [An exhibition of 12 watercolors by Cummings and 8 sculptures by Jorgensen] (New York: Painters & Sculptors Gallery, December 1–31, 1932), pp. [2]–[3].

C7 [Part of a Letter to William Rose Benét]. In *Fifty Poets: An American Auto-Anthology*, edited by William Rose Benét. New York: Duffield and Green, 1933, "Introduction", p. viii.

A reply to Benét's request for a contribution to his anthology. A drawing of an elephant that accompanied the reply is reproduced on page ix.

Reprinted in "Books and Things", by Isabel Paterson, New York *Herald Tribune*, xciii. 31,627 (Monday, June 19, 1933), 11.

C8 [SIX POEMS]. In *Modern Things*, edited by Parker Tyler. New York: The Galleon Press, 1934, pp. 22–28.

Contents: One. 'be of love(a little)'—Two. 'one nonsufficiently inunderstood'—Three. 'go(perpe)go'—Four. 'little joe gould has lost his teeth and doesn't know where'—Five. 'as if as'—Six. 'here's to opening and upward,to leaf and to sap'.

C9 Speech (from a forthcoming play). In *New American Caravan*, edited by Alfred Kreymborg, Lewis Mumford and Paul Rosenfeld. New York: W. W. Norton & Company, 1936, pp. 476–477.

Reprinted as "Speech: 1".

C10 THREE POEMS. In *New Directions in Prose and Poetry*, edited by James Laughlin IV. Norfolk, Conn.: New Directions, 1936, [*unpaged*].

Contents: 1. 'lucky means finding'—2. 'my specialty is living said'—3. 'economic secu'.

C11 SEVEN POEMS. In *New Directions in Prose & Poetry 1937*, edited by James Laughlin IV. Norfolk, Conn.: New Directions, 1937, [*unpaged*].

Contents: 1. 'hanged'—2. ' &-moon-He-be-hind-a-mills'—3. 'kind)'—4. 'porky & porkie'—5. 'The Mind's('—6. 'this little bride & groom are'—7. 'if i'.

C12 Ezra Pound. In *We Moderns* (Catalogue No. 42). New York: The Gotham Book Mart, 1940, p. 54.

Reprinted as "Anno Domini 1940".

C13 Speech from a Play [with part of a letter from Cummings explaining "Why he selected 'Speech from a Play' "]. In *This Is My Best*, edited by Whit Burnett. New York: The Dial Press, 1942, pp. 812–817.

Reprinted as "Speech: iii".

C : Various Contributions

C14 EIGHT POEMS. In *New Poems 1943*, edited by Oscar Williams. New York: Howell, Soskin, Publishers, 1943, pp. 72–76.

Contents: 1. 'old mr ly'—2. 'applaws)'—3. 'a salesman is an it that stinks Excuse'—4. 'a politician is an arse upon'—5. 'ygUDuh'—6. 'mr u will not be missed'—7. 'pity this busy monster,manunkind,'—8. 'darling!because my blood can sing'.

C15 Foreword. In *E. E. C's* [a facsimile of the artist's signature] [An exhibition of 45 oils and 15 watercolors]. New York: American British Art Center, March 1–18, 1944, p. [4].

This "catalogue" also contains reproductions of two oils by Cummings entitled "Evening"—reprinted in *Art News*, XLIII. 3 (March 15, 1944), 20—and "Selfportrait"—reprinted on the dust jacket of *1 × 1* and elsewhere.

Reprinted as "Foreword To Catalogue for an Exhibition of Cummings' Paintings".

C16 foreword. In *e. e. cummings* [An exhibition of 43 oils, 8 watercolors and 2 drawings]. Rochester, N.Y.: Rochester Memorial Gallery, 1945, p. [2].

Reprinted as "Foreword: 1".

C17 Is Something Wrong. In *The War Poets: An Anthology of the War Poetry of the 20th Century*, edited with an introduction by Oscar Williams. New York: The John Day Company, 1945, pp. 12–13.

Reprinted in *A Little Treasury of Modern Poetry: English and American* (Revised Edition), edited with an introduction by Oscar Williams (New York: Charles Scribner's Sons, 1952), pp. 815–816.

The War Poets also contains reprints of poems from *Is 5*, *ViVa* and *1 × 1*.

C18 Speech from a Forthcoming Play. In *The Partisan Reader—Ten Years of Partisan Review 1934–1944: An Anthology*, edited by William Phillips and Philip Rahv; introduction by Lionel Trilling. New York: The Dial Press, 1946, pp. 223–224.

Reprinted as "Speech: 11".

C19 Introduction. In *Krazy Kat*, by George Herriman. New York: Henry Holt and Company, 1946, [*unpaged*].

C20 By E. E. Cummings from *The Dial*, Vol. LXVIII, February, 1920. In *Gaston Lachaise 1882–1935, Exhibition*. New York: M. Knoedler & Co., January 20–February 15, 1947, pp. 7–9.

C21 SEVEN POEMS. In *Focus Four: The Novelist As Thinker*, edited by B. Rajan. London: Dennis Dobson Ltd., 1947, pp. 112–116.

Contents: 1. 'quick i the death of thing'—2. 'F is for foetus(a'—3. 'a kike is the most dangerous'—4. 'where's Jack Was'—5.

'why must itself up every of a park'—6. 'no time ago'—7. '(nothing whichful about'.

C22 Re Ezra Pound. In *The Case of Ezra Pound*, by Charles Norman. New York: The Bodley Press, 1948, pp. 46–47.

C23 [POEM]. In *Paul Rosenfeld, Voyager in the Arts*, edited by Jerome Mellquist and Lucie Wiese. New York: Creative Age Press, 1948, pp. 262–263.
　　First line: 'o// the round'.

C24 [Speaker's Text]. In *Œdipus Rex: Opera-Oratorio in two acts after Sophocles* (New revision 1948; Reduction for voice and piano by the composer), by Igor Strawinsky and Jean Cocteau. London: Edition Russe de Musique, Boosey & Hawkes, 1949.
　　Cummings' translation of the "Speaker's Text" was commissioned by The Juilliard Opera Theatre. It is printed on both sides of a single sheet of board and laid in the vocal score.

C25 [Foreword]. In *E. E. Cummings* [An exhibition of 38 oils, 11 watercolors and 2 drawings]. New York: American British Art Center, May 12–28, 1949, p. [2].
　　Reprint as "Foreword: II".

C26 [FOUR POEMS]. In *The Harvard Advocate Anthology*, edited by Donald Hall. New York: Twayne Publishers, Inc., 1950, pp. 135–138.
　　Contents: OF NICOLETTE ('Dreaming in marble all the palace lay,') —SUNSET ('Great carnal mountains crouching in the cloud')— SUMMER SILENCE (SPENSERIAN STANZA) ('Eruptive lightnings flutter to and fro')—BALLADE ('The white night roared with a huge north-wind').

C27 [A Letter to the Drama Editor of the New York *Times*]. In *In Memory of FITZI: March 16, 1877–March 30, 1955*. New York: Pauline Turkel, 1955, p. [4].
　　A pamphlet of tributes to the memory of M. Eleanor Fitzgerald, Director of the Provincetown Players.

C28 BEING TO TIMELESSNESS AS IT'S TO TIME. In *The New Pocket Anthology of American Verse*, edited by Oscar Williams. New York: Pocket Books, Inc., 1955, p. 128.
　　First line: 'being to timelessness as it's to time'.
　　Also as issued in a cloth bound edition by The World Publishing Company, Cleveland, 1955, p. 132.

C29 [A Note about Gaston Lachaise]. New York: Weyhe Gallery, December 27, 1955–January 28, 1956.
　　This untitled note is printed on one side of a single sheet of note-

size paper which was used as an announcement for an exhibition of drawings and sculpture by Lachaise.

C30 [Foreword]. In *e. e. cummings* [An exhibition of 19 paintings and drawings]. Rochester, N.Y.: University of Rochester, Fine Arts Gallery, April 1957.

This "catalogue" also reproduces a line drawing of a draped female nude by Cummings on the front cover.

Reprint as "Foreword: III".

C31 [THREE POEMS]. In *New Poems by American Poets #2*, edited by Rolfe Humphries. New York: Ballantine Books, 1957, pp. 38-39.

Contents: 'noone and a star stand,am to am'—'maggie and milly and molly and may'—'i am a little church(no great cathedral)'.

This anthology was issued in a paperback and cloth bound edition.

C32 [Poems, letters, telegrams, drawings, interviews, etc.]. In *The Magic Maker: E. E. Cummings*, by Charles Norman. New York: The Macmillan Company, 1958.

In addition to previously unpublished letters, notes, telegrams, drawings, etc., Mr. Norman's biography contains the following published, but uncollected, items: (p. 35) VISION ('The dim deep of a yellow evening slides')—(p. 36) SUMMER SILENCE (SPENSERIAN STANZA) ('Eruptive lightnings flutter to and fro')—(p. 40) SAPPHICS ('When my life his pillar has raised to heaven,')—(p. 40) HOKKU ('I care not greatly')—(pp. 41-42) NIGHT ('Night, with sunset hauntings;')—(p. 64) FINIS ('Over silent waters/ day descending/ night ascending')—(p. 186) [Part of a Letter to William Rose Benét]—(pp. 238-239) ["Warning": A note to the Provincetown Playhouse production of *Him*]—(p. 286) [Letter to the Editors of *Contempo*]—(p. 326) [A Letter to the Editors in] War Writers on Democracy—(p. 337) [A Statement in] Poets Here Scorn Soviet Attack on Work—(p. 348) [A "Communication" about Dylan Thomas]

D

Translations into Foreign Languages
of Books, Poems, and Essays

Translations of Cummings' poems by Octavio Paz into Spanish and Augusto de Campo into Portuguese have been published in periodicals in Mexico and Brazil respectively. However, all attempts to verify these appearances have proved unsuccessful.

I have been informed that all the translations into French credited to D. Jon Grossman and Alain Bosquet were originally the work of Mr. Grossman. The published versions, edited and reworked by Mr. Bosquet, were printed without the final approval of Mr. Grossman, Cummings' authorized French translator.

D

Translations into Foreign Languages
of Books, Poems, and Essays

ARABIC

ANTHOLOGY:

D1 [THREE POEMS]. In *Diwan Asher Al Ameriki,* jamaho wa nakalarho ela al aribia Yussef Khal. Beirut: Dai Majallat Sher, 1958, pp. 170–175.
   Contents: 1. 'All in green went my love riding'—2. 'the hours rise up putting off stars and it is'—3. 'you shall above all things be glad and young.'.

BENGALI

PERIODICAL:

D2 [TWO POEMS]. *Kavita* (Calcutta), XVI. 1 (December 1950), 38–41. Translations by Buddhadeva Bose. English and Bengali on opposite pages.
   Contents: 'when god lets my body be'—'O sweet spontaneous'.

DANISH

PERIODICAL:

D3 TO SONETTER. *Hvedekorn,* Year 33, no. 3 (May 1959), 117. Translations by Elsa Gress Wright.
   Contents: 1. 'if i should sleep with a lady called death'—II. 'it is funny, you will be dead some day.'.

E. E. Cummings

FRENCH

BOOK:

D3*a* *En traduction: Vingt-trois poèmes*. Choisis, traduits et présentés par D. Jon Grossman. Paris: Pierre Seghers, 1960. English and French on opposite pages.

    Contents: Introduction, by D. Jon Grossman—I. 'the hours rise up putting off stars and it is'—II. 'in Just-'—III. 'Picasso'—IV. 'Humanity i love you'—V. 'suppose'—VI. 'of this sunset (which is so'—VII. 'impossibly'—VIII. 'death is more than'—IX. 'Who knows if the moon's'—X. 'mr youse needn't be so spry' —XI. 'i am a beggar always'—XII. ODE ('o// the sweet & aged people')—XIII. ITEM ('this man is o so')—XIV. 'my sweet old etcetera'—XV. 'along the brittle treacherous bright streets'— XVI. 'kumrads die because they're told)'—XVII. 'he does not have to feel because he thinks'—XVIII. 'come(all you mischief-'— XIX. 'may my heart always be open to little'—XX. 'no man,if men are gods;but if gods must'—XXI. 'a politician is an arse upon' —XXII. 'why must itself up every of a park'—XXIII. 'in'.

ANTHOLOGIES:

D4 IMPRESSIONS IV. In *Anthologie de la nouvelle poésie américaine*, par Eugène Jolas. Paris: Simon Kra, 1928, pp. [50]–51.
    First line: 'the hours rise up putting off stars and it is'.

D5 [FOUR POEMS]. In *Écrivains et poètes des États-Unis d'Amérique*. Paris: Éditions de la Revue Fontaine, 1945, pp. [191]–193.
    A reprint of "Revue Fontaine, Éditions d'Alger, Aout 1943". See D12. Translations by Jean Wahl.

D6 [POEM]. In *Anthologie de la poésie américaine contemporaine*, par Maurice Le Breton. Paris: Les Éditions Denoël/, 1947, pp. 298–299. English and French on opposite pages.
    First line: 'when god lets my body be'.

D7 [SIX POEMS]. In *Panorama de la littérature contemporaine aux États-Unis*, par John Brown. Paris: Librairie Gallimard, 1954, pp. 504–511. The first, second, third and sixth poems translated by D. Jon Grossman and Alain Bosquet, and the fourth and fifth by Jeannie Chauveau and John Brown. English and French on opposite pages.
    Contents: 'the Cambridge ladies who live in furnished souls'— 'If you can't eat you got to'—'little man'—'all ignorance to-

boggans into know'—'darling!because my blood can sing'—
'when serpents bargain for the right to squirm'.

D8 [SIX POEMS]. In *Anthologie de la poésie américaine*, par Alain Bosquet.
Paris: Librairie Stock, Delamain et Boutelleau, 1956, pp. 196–
199. Translations by D. Jon Grossman and Alain Bosquet. English
and French on opposite pages.

    Contents: 'Buffalo Bill 's'—'little man'—'up into the silence
the green'—'these children singing in stone a'—'If you can't
eat you got to'—'when serpents bargain for the right to squirm'.

D9 [FOUR POEMS]. In *Les meilleurs poèmes anglais et américains
d'aujourd'hui*, [edited and translated by] Paul Ginestier. Paris:
Société d'Édition d'Enseignement Supérieur, 1958, pp. 152–155,
282–283, 304–305, 318–319. English and French on opposite pages.

    Contents: 'she being Brand'—'my love'—'o by the by'—
'here's a little mouse)and'.

PERIODICALS:

D10 Sipliss. *Le Navire d'Argent*. II. 10 (March 1, 1926), [195]–209.
A translation by Georges Duplaix of Chapter x, "Surplice", of
The Enormous Room.

D11 SONNET REALITIES. *le Journal des Poètes* (Brussels, Belgium), III.
4 (December 4, 1932), [4]. Translation by Florence Gilliam and
Jacques Baron.

    First line: '"kitty".   sixteen, 5' 1'', white, prostitute.'.

D12 [FOUR POEMS]. *Fontaine*, no. 27/28 (June/July 1943), [191]–193.
Translations by Jean Wahl.

    Contents: 'love is the every only god'—'i am so glad and very'
—'it may not always be so; and i say'—'the hours rise up putting
off stars and it is'.

D13 SEPT POÈMES. *Deucalion*, no. 4 (October 1952), [200]–207. Translations by D. Jon Grossman.

    Contents: 1. 'when my love comes to see me it's'—2. 'since
feeling is first'—3. 'O Distinct'—4. 'if there are any heavens
my mother will(all by herself)have'—5. 'little man'—6. 'love
is a place'—7. 'i thank You God for most this amazing'.

D14 DOUZE POÈMES. *Profils*, no. 2 (January 1953), [34]–49. Translations by D. Jon Grossman and Alain Bosquet. English and French
on opposite pages.

    Contents: I. 'Buffalo Bill 's'—II. 'little tree'—III. 'the Cam-
bridge ladies who live in furnished souls'—IV. 'twentyseven
bums give a prostitute the once'—V. 'in spite of everything'—

vi. 'worshipping Same'—vii. 'little man'—viii. 'up into the silence the green'—ix. 'these children singing in stone a'—x. 'If you can't eat you got to'—xi. 'out of the mountain of his soul comes'—xii. 'when serpents bargain for the right to squirm'.

Profils is the French edition of *Perspectives USA*.

D15 TROIS POÈMES. *l'Arc*, i. 3 (July 1958), 3–6. Translations by D. Jon Grossman.

Contents: i. '(ponder,darling,these busted statues'—ii. 'a/mong crum/bling people(a'—iii. 'these children singing in stone a'.

D16 [TEN POEMS]. *Europe: Revue Mensuelle* ("Literature des États-Unis"), Year 37, no. 358/359 (February/March 1959), 132–140. Translations by Renaud de Jouvenel.

Contents: Introduction, by Renaud de Jouvenel [contains a translation of '(fea']—'i spoke to thee'—'listen// beloved'—'beyond the brittle towns asleep'—'the moon is hiding in'—'my love is building a building'—'little ladies more'—'supposing i dreamed this)'—'you are like the snow only'—'may i feel said he'.

D17 POÈMES. *Les lettres nouvelles*, New Series, vii. 21 (September 16, 1959), 41–45. Translations by Mario Maurin.

Contents: 'to stand(alone)in some'—'now air is air and thing is thing:no bliss'—'maggie and milly and molly and may'—'un(bee)mo'—'joys faces friends'—THANKSGIVING (1956) ('a monstering horror swallows')—'here's s'.

GERMAN

BOOKS:

D18 *Der Endlose Raum*. Stuttgart: Victoria Verlag Martha Koerner, 1954. An authorized translation by Helmut M. Braem and Elisabeth Kaiser of *The Enormous Room*.

D19 *e. e. cummings·gedichte*. Munich: Langewiesche-Brandt, 1958. Translations by Eva Hesse. English and German on opposite pages. Edition issued in cloth and paper bindings.

Contents: 1. 'pity this busy monster,manunkind,'—2. 'may my heart always be open to little'—3. 'the hours rise up putting off stars and it is'—4. 'it really must'—5. ODE ('o// the sweet & aged people')—6. 'why must itself up every of a park'—7. 'my sweet old etcetera'—8. '"next to of course god america i'—9. 'come, gaze with me upon this dome'—10. 'the bigness of cannon'—11. 'plato told'—12. 'Humanity i love you'—13. 'any-

D : Translations

one lived in a pretty how town'—14. 'O sweet spontaneous'—
15. 'in Just-'—16. 'at the head of this street a gasping organ
is waving moth-'—17. 'Nobody wears a yellow'—18. 'All in
green went my love riding'—19. 'my darling since'—20. 'Thy
fingers make early flowers of'—21. 'my love'—22. 'i like my
body when it is with your'—23. 'the moon is hiding in'—
24. 'love is more thicker than forget'—25. 'somewhere i have
never travelled,gladly beyond'—26. 'Lady of silence'—27. 'what
if a much of a which of a wind'—28. 'i will wade out/ till my
thighs are steeped in burning flowers'—Nachwort, by Eva Hesse
[contains a translation of 'r-p-o-p-h-e-s-s-a-g-r'].

ANTHOLOGIES:

D20 "KEIN MITLEID DIESEM MONSTRUM IM BETRIEB". In *Gedichte von
Shakespeare bis Ezra Pound*, einführungen, urtexte und über-
tragungen [von] Hans Henneske. Wiesbaden: Limes Verlag,
1955, pp. 342–343. English and German on opposite pages.
First line: 'pity this busy monster,manunkind,'.

D21 [FOUR POEMS]. In *Gedichte Aus Der Neuen Welt: Amerikanische Lyrik
Seit 1910*, eingeleitet und übertragen von Kurt Heinrich Hansen.
Munich: R. Piper & Co. Verlag, 1956, pp. 7–8, 21, 38–39, 57.
Contents: 'the hours rise up putting off stars and it is'—'Paris;
this April sunset completely utters'—'listen// beloved'—'some-
where i have never travelled,gladly beyond'.

PERIODICALS:

D22 Einleitung. *Perspektiven*, no. 2 (January 1953), [37]–39. A trans-
lation by Alexander Koval of the "Introduction" to *Collected
Poems*.
Perspektiven is the German edition of *Perspectives USA*.

D23 AUSGEWÄHLTE GEDICHTE. *Perspektiven*, no. 2 (January 1953), [40]–
61. Translations by Alexander Koval and Kurt Erich Meurer.
English and German on opposite pages.
Contents: 'twentyseven bums give a prostitute the once'—'the
Cambridge ladies who live in furnished souls'—'Buffalo Bill 's'
—'little tree'—'if there are any heavens my mother will(all by
herself)have'—'in spite of everything'—'love is a place'—
'there is a here and'—'wherelings whenlings'—'these children
singing in stone a'—'up into the silence the green'—'love is more
thicker than forget'—'out of the mountain of his soul comes'
—'when serpents bargain for the right to squirm'.

E. E. Cummings

D24 GEDICHTE. *Wort und Wahrheit*, no. 5 (May 1957), 339, 340, 358, 364, 376. Translations by Franz Josef Sailer. German and English on the same page.

Contents: 'no time ago'—'i thank You God for most this amazing'—'i like'—'who were so dark of heart they might not speak'—'if there are any heavens my mother will(all by herself)have'.

D25 (FOUR POEMS in) E. E. Cummings oder Die Sprache, in der man nicht lugen kann, [von] Erich Fried. *Texte und Zeichen: Eine literarische Zeitschrift*, III. 5—no. 15 (September 15, 1957), 496–511. English followed by German.

Contents: 'the moon is hiding in'—'anyone lived in a pretty how town'—'my father moved through dooms of love'—'the hours rise up putting off stars and it is'.

ITALIAN

BOOK:

D26 *E. E. Cummings: Poesie Scelte*. Milano: All'Insegna del Pesce d'Oro, 1958. Translations by Salvatore Quasimodo. English and Italian on opposite pages. Edition limited to 1000 numbered copies.

Contents: Introduzione alle Poesie di E. E. Cummings, by Salvatore Quasimodo—1. 'this mind made war'—2. 'here is little Effie's head'—3. 'my girl's tall with hard long eyes'—4. 'love is a place'—5. 'you shall above all things be glad and young.'—6. 'as freedom is a breakfastfood'—7. 'wherelings whenlings'—8. 'anyone lived in a pretty how town'—9. 'my father moved through dooms of love'—10. 'these children singing in stone a'—11. 'love is more thicker than forget'—12. 'the great advantage of being alive'.

ANTHOLOGIES:

D27 DA SONNETTI-IRREALTÀ. In *Poeti Americani (1662–1945)*, a cura di Gabrielle Baldini. Torino: Francesco De Silva, 1949, pp. 394–395. English and Italian on opposite pages.

First line: 'it may not always be so; and i say'.

D28 315. In *Poeti Stranieri de '900: Tradotti da Poeti Italiani*, a cura di Vanni Scheiwiller. Milano: All'Insegna del Pesce d'Oro, 1955, p. 124. Translation by Salvatore Quasimodo. Edition limited to 2000 numbered copies.

First line: 'you shall above all things be glad and young.'.

D : Translations

PERIODICALS:

D29 Prefazione dell'Autore alle Proprie Poesie. *Prospetti*, no. 2 (January 1953), [52]-53. A translation by Fernanda Pivano of the "Introduction" to *Collected Poems*.

   Prospetti is the Italian edition of *Perspectives USA*.

D30 UNDICI POESIE. *Prospetti*, no. 2 (January 1953), [54]-79. Translations by Salvatore Quasimodo. English and Italian on opposite pages.

   Contents: 'here is little Effie's head'—'my girl's tall with hard long eyes'—'love is a place'—'you shall above all things be glad and young.'—'as freedom is a breakfastfood'—'wherelings whenlings'—'anyone lived in a pretty how town'—'my father moved through dooms of love'—'these children singing in stone a'—'love is more thicker than forget'—'the great advantage of being alive'.

JAPANESE

BOOK:

D31 *Cummings Shishu.* Tokyo: Eureka (Kaigai no shijin sosho 3), 1958. Translations by Yasuo Fujitomi.

   Contents: Introduction, by Yasuo Fujitomi [contains a translation of 'the hours rise up putting off stars and it is']—'Tumbling-hair/ picker of buttercups/ violets'—'Doll's boy 's asleep'—'the moon is hiding in'—'stinging'—'into the strenuous briefness'—'the rose'—'somebody knew Lincoln somebody Xerxes'—'my love'—'Buffalo Bill 's'—'in Just-'—'(one!)'—'Spring is like a perhaps hand'—'Take for example this:'—'when my love comes to see me it's'—'my sonnet is A light goes on in'—'Humanity i love you'—'the/ sky/ was'—'why did you go'—'will out of the kindness of their hearts a few philosophers tell me'—'curtains part)'—'this young question mark man'—'Nobody wears a yellow'—'sunlight was over'—'nothing is more exactly terrible than'—'myself,walking in Dragon st'—'love is a place'—'snow)says!Says'—'little man'—'mOOn Over tOwns mOOn'—'Q:dwo'—'if i'—'!blac'—'If you can't eat you got to'—'up into the silence the green'—'(sitting in a tree-)'—'when god decided to invent'—'(once like a spark)'—'open green those'—'yes is a pleasant country:'—'one day a nigger'—'no time ago'—'(fea'—'tw'—'the little horse is newlY'—'now all the fingers of this tree(darling)have'—'let's,from some loud

E. E. Cummings

unworld's most rightful wrong'—'i am a little church(no great cathedral)'—Afterword, by Yasuo Fujitomi.

ANTHOLOGY:

D32 TULIPS AND CHIMNEYS. In *Seki Meishishu Taisei II: America*. Tokyo: Heibonsha Kan, 1959, pp. [341]-361. Translations by Ichiro Kono.

Contents: 1. '(thee will i praise between those rivers whose'— 2. 'Thy fingers make early flowers of'—3. 'Tumbling-hair/ picker of buttercups/ violets'—4. 'my love'—5. 'it is at moments after i have dreamed'—6. 'All in green went my love riding'— 7. 'god gloats upon Her stunning flesh. Upon'—8. 'when citied day with the sonorous homes'—9. 'listen// beloved'—10. 'of evident invisibles'—11. 'Doll's boy 's asleep'—12. 'by little accurate saints thickly which tread'—13. 'the hours rise up putting off stars and it is'—14. 'beyond the brittle towns asleep'— 15. 'Always before your voice my soul'—16. 'when god lets my body be'—17. 'a connotation of infinity'—18. 'the moon is hiding in'—19. 'the glory is fallen out of'—20. 'a wind has blown the rain away and blown'—21. 'O sweet spontaneous'— 22. 'but the other'—23. 'any man is wonderful'—24. 'hist whist' —25. 'stinging'—26. 'spring omnipotent goddess thou dost'— 27. 'at the head of this street a gasping organ is waving moth-' —28. 'the Cambridge ladies who live in furnished souls'—29. 'i was considering how'—30. 'in Just-' —31. 'Buffalo Bill 's'—32. 'ladies and gentlemen this little girl'—33. 'into the strenuous briefness'—34. '"kitty". sixteen, 5' 1'', white, prostitute.'— 35. 'goodby Betty, don't remember me'—36. 'the'—37. 'when you rang at Dick Mid's Place'—38. 'writhe and'—39. 'the bigness of cannon'—40. 'somebody knew Lincoln somebody Xerxes' —41. 'between nose-red gross'—42. 'the rose'—43. 'it may not always be so; and i say'—44. 'yours is the music for no instrument'—45. 'a thing most new complete fragile intense,'—46. 'my love is building a building'—47. 'notice the convulsed orange inch of moon'.

PERIODICALS:

D33 [THREE POEMS]. *Poet Lore* (Special American Poetry Issue), no. 4 (July 1954), 54–56. Translations by Yasuo Fujitomi.

Contents: 'Nobody wears a yellow'—'the/ sky/ was'—'my-self,walking in Dragon st'.

D : Translations

D34 [FOUR POEMS]. *Sento*, no. 26 (August 1956), 10–15. Translations by Yasuo Fujitomi.

Contents: 'suppose'—'my sonnet is A light goes on in'—'why did you go'—'will out of the kindness of their hearts a few philosophers tell me'.

D35 THREE POEMS. *Sento*, no. 29 (June 1957), 14–20. Translations by Yasuo Fujitomi.

Contents: 'into the strenuous briefness'—'if i'—'sunlight was over'.

D36 TWO POEMS. *Sento*, no. 30 (October 1957), 14–16. Translations by Yasuo Fujitomi.

Contents: 'stinging'—'my love'.

D37 FOUR POEMS. *Sento*, no. 31 (February 1958), 17–19. Translations by Yasuo Fujitomi.

Contents: 'lucky means finding'—'Q:dwo'—'the wind is a Lady with'—'(one!)'.

D38 [POEM IN] E. E. Cummings, by Yasuo Fujitomi. *Sento*, no. 32 (May 1958), 1–4.

First line: 'the hours rise up putting off stars and it is'.

D39 TWO POEMS FROM 50 POEMS (1940). *Sento*, no. 32 (May 1958), 5–6. Translations by Yasuo Fujitomi.

Contents: ' !blac'—'If you can't eat you got to'.

NORWEGIAN

ANTHOLOGY:

D40 [SEVEN POEMS]. In *Amerikansk Lyrikk*, et utvalg i norsk gjendikt-ning ved Paal Brekke. Oslo: H. Aschehoug & Co. (W. Nygaard), 1957, pp. 104–110.

Contents: 'pity this busy monster,manunkind,'—'this little bride & groom are'—'in Just-'—'somewhere i have never travelled,gladly beyond'—'of evident invisibles'—'O sweet spontaneous'—'my sweet old etcetera'.

PERSIAN

ANTHOLOGY:

D41 AI ZAMIN BARVAR. In *Montakhebi Az Behtarin Achar Emrikai As 25 Shaer Maaroof Emrika As Gharn Hefdahom Ta Emrooz*, tardjomeh Shojaeldin Shafa ba moghadammeh dar bareh shehr va adab

E. E. Cummings

Emrikai be ghalame motardjam. Tehran: Ebnesina Publishing
Company, 1957, p. [91].
First line: 'O sweet spontaneous'.

PORTUGUESE

PERIODICALS:

D42 ["Foreword", "Introduction" and TWO POEMS in] Approach:
E. E. Cummings, by Judith Grossmann. *Jornal do Brasil* (Rio de
Janeiro), Suplemento Dominical (December 22, 1957), 4-5.
Contents: Foreword (*Is 5*)—Introduction (*Collected Poems*)—'i
think you like"'—'how// tinily'.

D43 APPROACH (2): E. E. CUMMINGS: SETE POEMAS. *Jornal do Brasil* (Rio
de Janeiro), Suplemento Dominical (January 12, 1958), 4-5.
Translations by Judith Grossmann.
Contents: POEM, OR BEAUTY HURTS MR. VINAL ('take it from me
kiddo')—'Buffalo Bill 's'—ITEM ('this man is o so')—'in Just-'
—'O sweet spontaneous'—'since feeling is first'—'somewhere i
have never travelled,gladly beyond'.

SPANISH

ANTHOLOGIES:

D44 Jean Le Nègre. In *Antología de Escritores Contemporáneos de los
Estados Unidos*, prosa y verso compliados por John Peale Bishop
y Allen Tate, versión de la prosa a cargo de Ricardo A. Latcham,
versión de la poesía a cargo de varios traductores. Santiago,
Chile: Editorial Nascimento, 1944, Volume II, pp. [7]-30. A
translation by Latcham of Chapter XI of *The Enormous Room*.

D45 [THREE POEMS]. In *La Poesía Inglesa: Los Contemporáneos*, selección,
traducción y prólogo de M. Manent. Barcelona: Ediciones Lauro,
1948, pp. 250-255. English and Spanish on opposite pages.
Contents: 'when god lets my body be'—'Thy fingers make early
flowers of'—'somewhere i hae never travelled,gladly beyond'.

D46 [FOUR POEMS]. In *Antología de la Poesía Norteamericana Contempo-
ránea*, selección, traducción y estudio preliminar de Eugenio
Florit. Washington, D.C.: Union Panamericana, 1955, pp. 95-
99. English and Spanish on opposite pages.
Contents: 'since feeling is first'—MEMORABILIA ('stop look &')
—'somewhere i have never travelled,gladly beyond'—'now all
the fingers of this tree(darling)have'.

D47 [POEM]. In *Diez Poetas Norteamericanos*, [translations by] Julian

D : Translations

Palley y A. A. Roggiano. Montevideo, Uruguay: Cuadernos Julio Herrera y Ressig (No. 4), 1955, p. [8].
First line: 'if i have made,my lady,intricate'.

PERIODICALS:.

D48 [TWO POEMS]. *Sur* (Buenos Aires), XIV. 113/114 (March/April 1944), [86]–[89]. Translations by A. Bioy Casares and J. L. Borges. English and Spanish on opposite pages.
Contents: 'Buffalo Bill 's'—'somewhere i have never travelled, gladly beyond'.

SWEDISH

ANTHOLOGY:

D49 [THIRTY-ONE POEMS in] Cummings, Med Några Kommentarer. In *Sidor av Amerika: Intryck och Resonemang*, av Thorsten Jonsson. Stockholm: Albert Bonniers Förlag, 1946, pp. 255–289.
Contents: 1. 'the Cambridge ladies who live in furnished souls' —2. 'somebody knew Lincoln somebody Xerxes'—3. 'memory believes'—4. 'if there are any heavens my mother will(all by herself)have'—5. 'in Just-'—6. 'when/ from a sidewalk/ out of(blown never quite to'—7. 'Spring is like a perhaps hand'— 8. ITEM ('this man is o so')—9. ? ('why are these pipples taking their hets off?')—10. 'the moon looked into my window'—11. 'the wind is a Lady with'—12. 'i will cultivate within'—13. 'one(Floatingly)arrive'—14. 'my sweet old etcetera'—15. 'look at this)'—16. 'her'—17. 'i like my body when it is with your' —18. 'it is so long since my heart has been with yours'—19. 'some ask praise of their fellows'—20. 'after all white horses are in bed'—21. 'what time is it i wonder never mind'—22. 'some-where i have never travelled,gladly beyond'—23. 'because i love you)last night'—24. 'lady will you come with me into'—25. 'be of love(a little)'—26. 'the glory is fallen out of'—27. 'into a truly'—28. 'silent unday by silently not night'—29. '("fire stop thief help murder save the world"'—30. 'may my heart always be open to little'—31. 'open your heart:'.

TURKISH

ANTHOLOGY:

D50 [TWO POEMS]. In *Çağdaş Amerikan Şiirleri*, Özdemir Nutku ile Tarık Dursun K., hazırlayıt türkçeleştirmiştir; Robert H. Ball 'un bir öndeyişi ile. Ankara: Sairler Yaprağı, 1956, pp. 19–20.

E. E. Cummings

Contents: 'somewhere i have never travelled,gladly beyond'—
'Paris; this April sunset completely utters'.

YIDDISH

ANTHOLOGY:

D51 LIED. In *Modern American Poetry*, translations by Michel Licht.
Buenos Aires: Julio Kaufman, 1954, p. 65.
First line: 'poets yeggs and thirsties'.

E

Musical Settings of Poems

E

Musical Settings of Poems

E1 Jimmie's got a goil. Musical setting by Marc Blitzstein for voice
and piano. In *Cos Cob Song Volume* (New York: Cos Cob Press, Inc.,
1935), pp. 17–19.
First line: 'Jimmie's got a goil/ goil/ goil,/ Jimmie'.
Also as reissued under the auspices of Arrow Music Press, Inc.,
1944.

E2 Song. Musical setting by Aaron Copland for voice and piano. In
Cos Cob Song Volume (New York: Cos Cob Press, Inc., 1935), pp.
20–25.
First line: 'in spite of everything'.
Also as reissued under the auspices of Arrow Music Press, Inc.,
1944.

E3 *Chanson Innocentes*. Musical settings by Lehman Engel for women's
chorus (three-part) and piano. New York: Arrow Music Press,
Inc., 1939.
Contents: 1. 'in Just-'—11. 'hist   whist'—111. 'Tumbling-
hair/ picker of buttercups/ violets'.

E4 *This Is the Garden*. Musical setting by David Diamond for chorus
of mixed voices (four-part, a cappella). New York: Carl Fischer,
Inc., 1940.
First line: 'this is the garden: colours come and go,'.

E5 *Four Uncles*. Musical setting by David Diamond for voice and
piano. Philadelphia, Pa.: Elkan-Vogel Co., Inc., 1946.
First line: 'my uncle'.

E6 *Six Songs*. Musical settings by William Bergsma for voice and
piano. New York: Carl Fischer, Inc., 1947.
Contents: 1. 'when god lets my body be'—11. 'Doll's boy 's

E. E. Cummings

asleep'—III. 'hist   whist'—IV. 'Thy fingers make early flowers of'—V. 'it may not always be so; and i say'—VI. 'Jimmie's got a goil/ goil/ goil,/ Jimmie'.

E7 *Two Love Songs.* Musical settings by Everett Helm for medium voice and piano. New York: Music Press, Inc., 1947.

    Contents: It Is So Long ('it is so long since my heart has been with yours')—For My Lady ('if i have made,my lady,intricate').

E8 *sam was a man.* Musical setting by Vincent Persichetti for two-part chorus of mixed voices, women's or men's, with piano accompaniment. New York: G. Schirmer, Inc., 1948.

    First line: 'rain or hail'.

E9 *Tumbling-hair.* Musical setting by Peter Mennin for women's chorus (three-part) and piano. New York: Carl Fischer, Inc., 1949.

    First line: 'Tumbling-hair/ picker of buttercups/ violets'.

E10 *Jimmie's got a goil.* Musical setting by Vincent Persichetti for two-part chorus of mixed voices, women's or men's, with piano accompaniment. New York: G. Schirmer, Inc., 1949.

    First line: 'Jimmie's got a goil/ goil/ goil,/ Jimmie'.

E11 *All In Green Went My Love Riding.* Musical setting by David Diamond for women's chorus (three-part, a cappella). New York: Southern Music Publishing Co., Inc., 1950.

    First line: 'All in green went my love riding'.

E12 *The Glory Is Fallen Out of the Sky.* Musical setting by David Diamond for women's chorus (three-part, a cappella). New York: Southern Music Publishing Co., Inc., 1950.

    First line: 'the glory is fallen out of'.

E13 *If You Can't.* Musical setting by David Diamond for voice and piano. New York: Leeds Music Corp., 1950.

    First line: 'If you can't eat you got to'.

E14 *Hist Whist.* Musical setting by Vincent Persichetti for women's chorus (two-part, a cappella). New York: Carl Fischer, Inc., 1952.

    First line: 'hist   whist'.

E15 *This Is the Garden.* Musical setting by Vincent Persichetti for women's chorus (three-part, a cappella). New York: Carl Fischer, Inc., 1952.

    First line: 'this is the garden: colours come and go,'.

E16 My Sweet Old Etcetera. Musical setting by Hugo Weisgall for baritone and piano. In *Soldier Songs* (New York: Mercury Music Corp., 1953), pp. 12–15.

    First line: 'my sweet old etcetera'.

E : Musical Settings

E17 *Love Is More*. Musical setting by David Diamond for voice and piano. New York: Southern Music Publishing Co., Inc., 1954.
First line: 'love is more thicker than forget'.

E18 *Just-Spring*. Musical setting by John Duke for voice and piano. New York: Carl Fischer, Inc., 1954.
First line: 'in Just-'.

E19 *The Mountains Are Dancing*. Musical setting by John Duke for voice and piano. New York: Carl Fischer, Inc., 1956.
First line: 'when faces called flowers float out of the ground'.

E20 *Anyone Lived in a Pretty How Town*. Musical setting by Charles Hamm for voice and piano. Northampton, Mass.: Valley Music Press, 1956.
First line: 'anyone lived in a pretty how town'.

E21 *A Definition*. Musical setting by Earl George for women's chorus (four-part, a cappella). New York: Lawson-Gould Music Publishers, Inc., 1956.
First line: 'love is more thicker than forget'.

E22 *anyone lived in a pretty how town*. Musical setting by Josef Alexander for chorus of mixed voices (four-part, a cappella). New York: Lawson-Gould Music Publishers, Inc., 1956.
First line: 'anyone lived in a pretty how town'.

E23 *My Sweet Old Etcetera*. Musical setting by Robert Starer for voice and piano. New York: Leeds Music Corp., 1957.
First line: 'my sweet old etcetera'.

E24 *hist . . . whist*. Musical setting by John Duke for voice and piano. New York: Southern Music Publishing Co., Inc., 1957.
First line: 'hist   whist'.

E25 *may my heart*. Musical setting by Serge de Gastyne for voice and piano. Philadelphia, Pa.: Elkan-Vogel Co., Inc., 1958.
First line: 'may my heart always be open to little'.

E26 *a pretty a day*. Musical setting by Karol Rathaus for mixed chorus (four-part, a cappella). Bryn Mawr, Pa.: Theodore Presser Company, 1959.
First line: 'a pretty a day'.

E27 *These Children Singing in Stone*. Musical setting by Paul Nordoff for voice and piano. New York: American Music Edition, 1960.
First line: 'these children singing in stone a'.

E28 *Sam*. Musical setting by Paul Nordoff for voice and piano. New York: American Music Edition, 1960.
First line: 'rain or hail'.

E. E. Cummings

E29 *Tumbling-Hair*. Musical setting by Paul Nordoff for voice and piano. New York: American Music Edition, 1960.

   First line: 'Tumbling-hair/ picker of buttercups/ violets'.

E30 *Little Tree*. Musical setting by Paul Nordoff for voice and piano. New York: American Music Edition, 1960.

   First line: 'little tree'.

F

Recorded Readings by E. E. Cummings

F

Recorded Readings by E. E. Cummings

F1 "*Seven Poems*" *by E. E. Cummings read by Mr. Cummings*. Decca Records, [*unnumbered*] (12" 78rpm), 1938.

Contents: Side One. POEM, OR BEAUTY HURTS MR. VINAL ('take it from me kiddo')—ITEM ('this man is o so')—'Buffalo Bill 's'; Side Two. 'in Just-'—'O sweet spontaneous'—'since feeling is first'—'somewhere i have never travelled,gladly beyond'.

This record was issued in cooperation with Harcourt, Brace and Company as a promotional piece for the publication of *Collected Poems*. It was later reissued by Educational Services, Washington, D.C., [*unnumbered*] (12" 78rpm), and the Linguaphone Institute, 76787 (12" 78rpm).

F2 *E. E. Cummings Reading from "50 Poems"*. The National Council of Teachers of English, Contemporary Poets Series 51–52 (10" 78rpm) 1942.

Contents: Side 51. 'proud of his scientific attitude'—'one slipslouch twi'—'love is more thicker than forget'; Side 52. 'anyone lived in a pretty how town'.

F3 *E. E. Cummings Reading His Own Poems*. The Library of Congress, Twentieth Century Poetry in English P 18 (12" 78rpm), 1947.

Contents: Side A. 'plato told'—'my father moved through dooms of love' (beginning); Side B. 'my father moved through dooms of love' (concluded).

Also as reissued by the Library of Congress, PL 5 (12" 33⅓rpm).

F4 E. E. Cummings. In *Pleasure Dome: An audible anthology of modern poetry read by its creators*, edited by Lloyd Frankenberg. Columbia Records, MM 877, record 72897D (12" 78rpm), 1949.

Contents: 'Spring is like a perhaps hand'—'this little bride &

groom are'—'pity this busy monster,manunkind,'—'rain or hail'.

Also as reissued by Columbia Records, ML 4259 (12″ 33⅓rpm).

F5 *E. E. Cummings Reads.* Caedmon Publishers, TC 1017 (12″ 33⅓rpm), 1953.

Contents: Side One. *Him*, the acrobat passage—*Eimi*, Lenin's tomb—*Santa Claus*, Scene Three; Side Two. 1. 'when serpents bargain for the right to squirm'—2. 'dying is fine)but Death'—3. 'why must itself up every of a park'—4. 'when god decided to invent'—5. 'nothing false and possible is love'—6. 'Hello is what a mirror says'—7. 'who were so dark of heart they might not speak,'—8. 'i say no world'—9. 'life is more true than reason will deceive'—10. 'what if a much of a which of a wind'—11. 'o by the by'—12. 'one's not half two. It's two are halves of one:'—13. 'hate blows a bubble of despair into'—14. 'yes is a pleasant country:'—15. 'i thank You God for most this amazing'—16. '"sweet spring is your'—17. 'true lovers in each happening of their hearts'—18. 'when faces called flowers float out of the ground'.

Poems 10 and 16 were reissued by Caedmon Publishers as part of *the caedmon treasury of modern poets reading*, TC 2006 (2 12″ 33⅓rpm).

G

Reproductions of Drawings, Watercolors, and Oils by E. E. Cummings

NOTE: In addition to the work collected in *CIOPW* and reproductions used to illustrate the author's texts, Cummings has contributed drawings, watercolors, and oils to periodicals for reproduction without text. This section lists, chronologically, these separate appearances.

G

Reproductions of Drawings, Watercolors, and Oils by E. E. Cummings

G1 National Winter Garden Burlesque I–IV [line drawings]. *The Dial*, LXVIII. 1 (January 1920), [26a]–[26d].

"National Winter Garden Burlesque [1]" reprinted in *The Seven Lively Arts*, by Gilbert Seldes (New York: Harper & Brothers, 1924), p. [294a]. Also reprinted as "Shargel".

G2 [Four Line Drawings]. *The Dial*, LXX. 1 (January 1921), [54a]–[54d].

The first drawing reprinted as "elephant".

G3 A Line Drawing. *The Dial*, LXXI. 2 (August 1921), [264a].

Reprinted as "knockout".

G4 [Four Line Drawings]. *The Dial*, LXXII. 1 (January 1922), [46a]–[46d].

G5 A Line Drawing. *The Dial*, LXXIII. 2 (August 1922), [132a].

Reprinted as "dancers".

G6 [Four Line Drawings]. *The Dial*, LXXIV. 1 (January 1923), [30a]–[30d].

G7 [An Oil Painting and Two Wash Drawings]. *The Dial*, LXXVI. 1 (January 1924), [32a]–[32c].

Contents: Portrait of the Artist [oil]—A Wash Drawing—Bullfight [wash drawing].

G8 Charles Spencer Chaplin [a line drawing]. *The Dial*, LXXVI. 3 (March 1924), [248a].

Reprinted as "Charlie Chaplin" in *The Seven Lively Arts*, by Gilbert Seldes (New York: Harper & Brothers, 1924), p. [42a].

E. E. Cummings

G9 Dancers [a line drawing]. *The Dial*, LXXVIII. 6 (June 1925), [464a].

G10 [Two Line Drawings]. *The Dial*, LXXIX. 4 (October 1925), [304a]–[304b].

G11 Noise Number 13 [oil]. *The Dial*, LXXXIII. 2 (August 1927), [122a].

G12 [Two Wash Drawings]. *The Dial*, LXXXIII. 6 (December 1927), [500a]–[500b].

The first drawing reprinted as "train". The subject of the second—Anne Barton and her daughter—appears in "portrait self".

G13 Bal Négre [a line drawing]. *This Quarter*, II. 1 (September 1929). [147].

G14 Drawing. *This Quarter*, v. 2 (December 1932), [319].

Indexes

Index to Titles and First Lines

of Cummings' Works

E. E. Cummings

E. E. Cummings

Cummings' Titles and First Lines

E. E. Cummings

Cummings' Titles and First Lines

E. E. Cummings

meet mr universe(who clean, A23, 25
Memorabilia, A6, 17, 25, 28; B55; D46
memory believes, A11, 17, 25; D49
Merrygoround, A10
might these be thrushes climbing through almost(do they, A19, 25; B130
mighty guest of merely me, A23, 25
Miracles and Dreams, A26; B91
A Miscellany, A26
Mist, B2
moan, A18, 25
A Modern Gulliver Explores the Movies, A26; B57
moon over gai, A14, 25
mOOn Over tOwns mOOn, A14, 17, 25; D31
Moonrise, A10
morsel miraculous and meaningless, A14, 17, 25
mortals), A18, 25; B120
most(people, A14, 17, 25
The Mountains Are Dancing, E19
mouse)Won, A14, 17, 25; B99
move, A14, 17, 25
mr u will not be missed, A19, 25; B129; C14
Mr. X, A26; B90
mr youse needn't be so spry, A6, 17, 25, 28; D3a
mrs, A18, 25
much i cannot), A14, 17, 25
murderfully in midmost o.c.an, A11, 25
Music, B3
Music is sweet from the thrush's throat!, B3
must being shall, A17, 25
my darling since, A11, 17, 25; B95; D19
my eyes are fond of the east side, A4, 25
my father moved through dooms of love, A18, 25, 28; D25–26, 30; F3
my girl's tall with hard long eyes, A3b–c, 4, 17, 25; D26, 30
my(his from daughter's mother's zero mind, A19, 25
my love, A3, 17, 25; B40; D9, 19, 31–32, 36

My love is building a building, B30
my love is building a building, A3, 17, 25; B30; D16, 32
my mind is, A3b–c, 5, 25
my naked lady framed, A3b–c, 4, 25
my smallheaded pearshaped, A4, 25; B46
my sonnet is A light goes on in, A3b–c, 4, 17, 25; D31, 34
my specialty is living said, A17, 25, 28; C10
my strength becoming wistful in a glib, A4, 25
My Sweet Old Etcetera, E16, 23
my sweet old etcetera, A6, 17, 25, 28; D3a, 19, 40, 49; E16, 23
my uncle, A6, 17, 25; E5
myself,walking in Dragon st, A11, 17, 25; D31, 33

n, A27; B191
Napoli, A10
National Winter Garden Burlesque I–IV, G1
nearer:breath of my breath:take not thy tingling, A3b–c, 4, 17, 25
Nederlands, A10
neither awake, A23, 25; B149
neither could say, A19, 25
never could anyone, A27
The New Art, A26; B17; C1
New Hampshire, Winter, A10
The New Mother Goose, A26; B89
New Poems (Collected Poems), A17, 25
New York, 1927, A10
newlys of silence, A18, 25
"next to of course god america i, A6, 17, 25, 28; B60; D19
Night, B12; C32
Night, with sunset hauntings;, B12; C32
nine birds(rising, A23, 25
Nine Poems, B111
95 Poems, A27
nite), B229
no man,if men are gods;but if gods must, A19, 25, 28; D3a
No sunset, but a grey, great, struggling sky, B14
No Thanks, A14, 16–17, 25; B112

E. E. Cummings

Cummings' Titles and First Lines

Take for example this:, A4, 17, 25; B41; D31

take it from me kiddo, A6, 17, 25, 28; B39; F1

tell me not how electricity or, A11, 25

Ten Poems, D16

than(by yon sunset's wintry glow, A6, 17, 25

Thanksgiving (1956), A27; B216; D17

that famous fatheads find that each, A14, 25

that melancholy, A27; B190

that which we who're alive in spite of mirrors, A14, 17, 25; B112

the, A3, 17, 25; D32

the bed is not very big, A4, 17, 25

the bigness of cannon, A3, 17, 25; B25; D19, 32

the boys i mean are not refined, A14*a*

the Cambridge ladies who live in furnished souls, A3, 17, 25, 28; B35; D7, 14, 23, 32, 49

The dim deep of a yellow evening slides, B1; C32

the dirty colours of her kiss have just, A4, 17, 25

the dress was a suspicious madder, importing the cruelty of roses., A3*b–c*, 4, 17, 25

the emperor, A3, 25

the first president to be loved by his, A11, 17, 25

The flute of morning stilled in noon—, B32

the glory is fallen out of, A3, 17, 25; D32, 49; E12

the great advantage of being alive, A23, 25, 28; D26, 30

the hills, A3*b–c*, 5, 25

the hours rise up putting off stars and it is, A3, 17, 25; D1, 3*a*, 4–5, 12, 19, 21, 25, 31–32, 38

the ivory performing rose, A3*b–c*, 4, 17, 25

the little horse is newlY, A23, 25; D31

the mind is its own beautiful prisoner., A4, 17, 25

The Mind's(, A17, 25; B116; C11

the moon is hiding in, A3, 17, 25; D16, 19, 25, 31–32

the moon looked into my window, A6, 16–17, 25; D49

the Noster was a ship of swank, A18, 25

the of an it ignoblest he, A23, 25; B155

the(oo)is, A27; B195

the people who, A17, 25

(the phonograph's voice like a keen spider skipping, A3*b–c*, 4, 25

the poem her belly marched through me as, A4, 17, 25

the rose, A3, 17, 25; D31–32

the season 'tis, my lovely lambs, A6, 17, 25; B44

the silently little blue elephant shyly(he was terri, A18, 25

the skinny voice, A3*b–c*, 5, 16–17, 25; B37

the sky a silver, A3, 25

the/ sky/ was, A3*b–c*, 5, 17, 25; D31, 33

the surely, A11, 25

the waddling, A3*b–c*, 4, 6, 25

the way to hump a cow is not, A18, 25

The white night roared with a huge north-wind, B7; C26

the wind is a Lady with, A4, 17, 25; B46; D37, 49

the(/Wistfully, A14, 25; B109

the young, A3, 25

The Theatre, B76–77

Theatre: I, A26; B76

Theatre: II, A26; B77

(thee will i praise between those rivers whose, A3, 17, 25; D32

there are possibly 2½ or impossibly 3, A18, 25; B123

there are 6 doors., A11, 17, 25

there is a, A3, 25

there is a here and, A18, 25; D23

These Children Singing in Stone, E27

these children singing in stone a, A18, 25, 28; B120; D8, 14–15, 23, 26, 30; E27

these from my mother's greatgrand-

Cummings' Titles and First Lines

upon the room's/ silence, i will sew, A4, 25

utterly and amusingly i am pash, A3*b–c*, 4, 17, 25

Vanity Fair's Prize Movie-Scenario, A26; B53

The Very Latest School in Art, A26; B67

Videlicet, A26; B203

Vision, B1; C32

W (ViVa), A11, 16–17, 25; B98; C17

Vive la Folie!, A26; B80

voices to voices, lip to lip, A6, 16–17, 25, 28; B50

W. H. W., Jr. In Memory of "A House of Pomegranates", B24

The Wanderer, A2

Warning (Program Note to Him), C3, 32

warped this perhapsy, A18, 25

A Wash Drawing, G7

Water-Lilies, B2

we love each other very dearly/, more, A19, 25

we miss you,jack—tactfully you(with one cocked, A23, 25; B161

we)under)over,the thing of floating Of, A14, 25

weazened Irrefutable unastonished, A6, 17, 25; B50

Weligion Is Hashish, A26; B105

well)here's looking at ourselves, A11, 17, 25

what a proud dreamhorse pulling(smoothloomingly)through, A14, 17, 25, 28

What About It?, A26; B119

What does little Ernest croon, B111

what does little Ernest croon, A14, 25; B111

what freedom's not some under's mere above, A18, 25, 28

what Got him was Noth, A27; B216

What If a Much, B130

what if a much of a which of a wind, A19, 25, 28; B130; D19; F5

what is strictly fiercely and wholly dies, A11, 25

What Our Loving Subscribers Say, A26; B54

what over and which under, A19, 25

what time is it i wonder never mind, A11, 17, 25; B97; D49

whatever's merely wilful, A27; B170

when an honest injum toma, B137

when any mortal(even the most odd), A27

When Calvin Coolidge Laughed, A26; B58

when cities day with the sonorous homes, A3, 17, 25; D32

when faces called flowers float out the ground, A23, 25, 28; B158; E19; F5

when/ from a sidewalk/ out of(blown never quite to, A14, 17, 25; D49

when god decided to invent, A19, 25, 28; B128; D31; F5

when god lets my body be, A3, 17, 25, 28; B25; D2, 6, 32, 45; E6

when hair falls off and eyes blur And, A11, 17, 25

when i am in Boston, i do not speak., A3*b–c*, 5, 17, 25

when i have thought of you some-what too, A4, 25

when learned darkness from our searched world, A3*b–c*, 5, 17, 25

when life is quite through with, A3*b–c*, 5, 17, 25; B25

when mack smacked phyllis on the snout, A27; B200

when muckers pimps and tratesmen, A14, 17, 25; B111

When my life his pillar has raised to heaven, B20; C32

when my love comes to see me it's, A3*b–c*, 4, 17, 25; D13, 31

when my sensational moments are no more, A3*b–c*, 5, 17, 25

When rain whom fear, B93

when rain whom fear, A11, 17, 25; B93

when serpents bargain for the right to squirm, A23, 25, 28; B159; D7–8, 14, 23; F5

E. E. Cummings

When the lithe moonlight silently, B10

when the proficient poison of sure sleep, A3*b–c*, 5, 17, 25

when the spent day begins to frail, A4, 17, 25; B46

When thou hast taken thy last applause, and when, A1

when thou hast taken thy last applause, and when, A1, 3, 25

when unto nights of autumn do complain, A3*b–c*, 5, 17, 25

)when what hugs stopping earth than silent is, A18, 25; B120

when you are silent,shining host by guest, A19, 25

when you rang at Dick Mid's Place, A3, 17, 25; B35; D32

when you rang at Dick Mid's place, B35

when you went away it was morning, A4, 25

when your honest redskin toma, A23, 25; B137

Where is my love! I cried., B16

whereas by dark really released, the modern, A3*b–c*, 4, 25

wherelings whenlings, A18, 25; D23, 26, 30

where's Jack Was, A23, 25; B145; C21

Where's Madge then, A3*b–c*, 5, 17, 25; B40

which is the very, A19, 25

whippoorwill this, A27

who(at, A27; B213

who before dying demands not rebirth, A14, 25

who(is?are)who, A27; B196

who is this, B228

who knows if the moon's, A4, 17, 25, 28; D3*a*

who sharpens every dull, A23, 25; B166

Who/ threw the silver dollar up into the tree?/ I didn't, A4, 25

who were so dark of heart they might not speak, A23, 25; B138; D24; F5

who's most afraid of death? thou, A3*b–c*, 5, 17, 25; B33

whose are these(wraith a clinging with a wraith), A23, 25; B149

why, A27

why are these pipples taking their hets off?, A6, 17, 25; B51; D49

why did you go, A3*b–c*, 5, 17, 25; D31, 34

why from this her and him, A27

Why I Like America, A26; B87

why must itself up every of a park, A23, 25; B145; C21; D3*a*, 19; F5

why why, A14, 25

Wien, A10

Will i ever forget that precarious moment?, A6, 17, 25; B48

will out of the kindness of their hearts a few philosophers tell me, A6, 17, 25; B41; D31, 34

will suddenly trees leap from winter and will, A3*b–c*, 5, 25

(will you teach a, A18, 25

William Adams-Wiggley: Genius and Christian, A26; B59

windows go orange in the slowly., A3*b–c*, 4, 25

Wing Wong,uninterred at twice, A11, 17, 25; B98

with breathing as (faithfully) her lownecked, A6, 17, 25; B45

Words into Pictures, A26; B163

workingman with hand so hairysturdy, A6, 25; B38

worshipping Same, A14, 17, 25; B111; D14

writhe and, A3, 17, 25; D32

y is a WELL KNOWN ATHLETE'S BRIDE, A11, 17, 25

Y.x, A10

yes but even, A27

yes is a pleasant country:, A19, 25, 28; D31; F5

ygUDuh, A19, 25; B129; C14

yonder deadfromtheneckup graduate of a, A6, 17, 25

you, A11, 17, 25; B93

you are like the snow only, A6, 17, 25; D16

you are not going to, dear. You are not going to and, A6, 17, 25

Cummings' Titles and First Lines

Index to Other Titles and Names

Other Titles and Names

Other Titles and Names

E. E. Cummings

Other Titles and Names

E. E. Cummings: A Bibliography
has been set in Monotype Garamond #248, and printed from
plates. The paper is Warren's Olde Style, white wove. The binding cloth is Holliston Roxite. Complete manufacture by The
Plimpton Press.

WESLEYAN UNIVERSITY PRESS
MIDDLETOWN, CONNECTICUT